100% OFFICIAL

JUSTIN BIEBER

First Step 2 Forever: My Story

HarperCollins Publishers

77–85 Fulham Palace Road

Hammersmith, London W6 8JB

www.harpercollins.co.uk

First published by HarperCollins Publishers 2010

1 3 5 7 9 10 8 6 4 2

A catalogue record of this book is available from the British Library

ISBN 978-0-00-790116-6

Printed in China by South China Printing Co. Ltd,

CONTENTS

A Special DM to the Greatest
Fans in the World! **7**

1 Let's Get This Show on the Road **9**

2 A Secret Musician **25**

3 The Stratford Star **65**

4 YouTube: My First Million **97**

5 The Start of a New Life **129**

6 Welcome to My World **167**

7 Just the Beginning **205**

Thank You **240**

A SPECIAL DM TO THE GREATEST FANS IN THE WORLD!

How can I begin to thank you for making this journey possible? Every one of you is 'My Favorite Girl' for a different reason, because each of you is special in your own way. Everywhere I go, whatever I do, I try to connect with as many of you as possible. If you're up front at a concert, I might reach out and hold your hand. If you show up outside the arena after the show, you might get soaked in one of our epic water fights. You might just be talking to your friends on Twitter saying you have a one-in-a-million chance of reaching me and now I'm following you. My dreams used to be a one-in-a-million chance as well, but as I said in the song, never say never. I never forget that none of this would have happened without you. That's why I want to share this story with you: so you can experience the journey with me, all the highs and lows, the laughter and the tears. You were there from the beginning. Now, as you see what I saw and feel what I felt, I hope you'll believe that big dreams really can come true. I'm living mine every day. Thanks to you.

LUV YAH,
JUSTIN

CHAPTER 1

LET'S GET THIS SHOW ON THE ROAD

justinbieber Canada thank u!! Sad I had 2 leave but we r starting the tour and had to get back to rehearsals . . . MY BUS RULES!! It's a party on wheels!

4:17 PM Jun 21st via web

HARTFORD, CONNECTICUT
TUESDAY, 22 JUNE 2010
9.45 A.M.

Rolling into the XL Center, I feel like I ought to have skates on my feet.

'Hey!' I elbow my grandpa in the ribs. 'Can't you just smell the hockey?'

He laughs. 'Oh, yeah.'

In less than forty hours, the XL Center will be jammed to the rafters with almost twenty thousand screaming fans, but right now the venue is just begging for a Zamboni.

A Zamboni is that huge tank-like thing they drive around to even out the ice during halftime at a hockey game. It melts the top layer, which almost immediately refreezes as smooth as glass. But I can't believe I have to describe what a Zamboni is. It's like describing something you've known since the day you were born.

"A lot can change in three years... it's unreal"

Being a Canadian, hockey is our thing. We have it in our blood.

Sometimes they let a celebrity guest – a war hero, beauty-pageant winner, local news anchor, or whatever – ride in the Zamboni. And, until three years ago, that was my definition of celebrity: somebody who gets to ride around in the Zamboni. My definition of a rock star was somebody who gets to ride around in a tour bus.

A lot can change in three years.

When I was twelve, my manager, Scott 'Scooter' Braun, saw a YouTube video of me performing in a local talent show. When I was fourteen, we joined forces with the recording artist Usher, who was not only one of my heroes but helped introduce me to the world. A few months after my fifteenth birthday, my first single dropped. Now I'm sixteen and about to launch my first tour as a headliner.

IT'S UNREAL.

The My World Tour will hit eighty-five cities in the US and Canada – connecting with almost two million fans – all in less than six months. My backup singers, Legaci, my dancers, band and a huge crew are all on the ride with me. It takes eight buses and a whole fleet of eighteen-wheelers to move all the people and equipment.

WOW!

"The My World Tour will hit eighty-five cities – connecting with almost two million fans – all in less than six months"

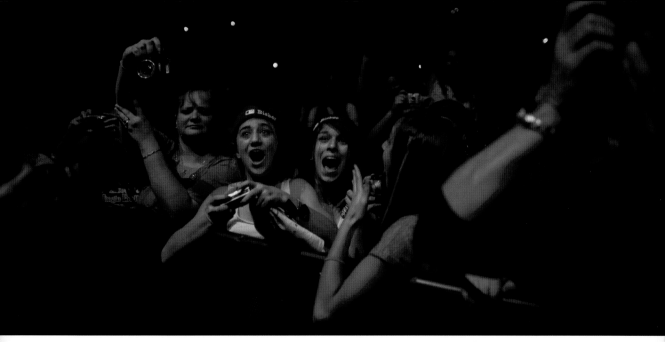

I make my way across the bus garage with my grandparents, Bruce and Diane Dale, and Kenny Hamilton, personal security ninja and frequent victim of my Xbox 360 powers of annihilation. My mom, Pattie Mallette, teeters along behind us, rocking skinny jeans and high heels. Mom is a trip and she sacrificed everything for me.

Scooter has already been at the venue for hours, shooting hoops with the roadies and backup dancers between frantic cellphone calls. Scooter's the mastermind behind the operation and he and the team wrestle all the details into place: media stuff, like interviews and photo requests; logistical stuff, like who's going where in which bus; and of course crucial life-dependent matters, like making sure I don't eat any pizza the day of the show (singers aren't supposed to have dairy before a show, but we all know I'm a rule breaker. Pizza is just so good!). Scooter's always strategizing – he treats life like chess, always eight moves ahead. The dude's a beast.

With a quick fist bump 'wassup' to Kenny and hugs for me and Mom, he leads us through the backstage catacombs to the arena where the tour riggers are craning in a huge steel-framed hot air balloon basket.

'Nice.' Kenny and I nod our approval.

This thing is designed to fly me out over the crowd during the song 'Up', starting upstage about thirty feet in the air, then floating out over their heads, gliding on waves of energy and noise, dipping not quite low enough for them to touch, but close enough for me to see all those beautiful faces. I really hope my fans are gonna go crazy when they see it. But then the gondola makes a noise like a Chevy grinding through a guardrail. It lurches to a halt. Jerks to the left. Wobbles to the right.

I'm like, 'Whoa, dude! That's not supposed to happen.'

High in the catwalks, the fly riggers debate back and forth on their walkie-talkies in hushed voices. Not cool. But, just when I start to experience some talkback from the big breakfast in my stomach, I feel a reassuring arm around my shoulders. Scooter's girlfriend, Carin, is standing beside me. Carin is helping out on tour – but really she is here to help me and Scooter navigate this crazy time in our lives. She's a major part of our support system, and always has my wellbeing at the front of her mind.

'Don't worry,' she says. 'It'll be cool. Safety comes way before special effects. You know that.'

'Yeah, I know,' I tell her. 'But I don't want to have to cut any of the tricks. The show is so awesome. I just want it to go perfect.'

'It will,' says Mom. 'It's going to be amazing.'

'Totally amazing,' Carin agrees. 'Look. I think they've got it.'

The steel gondola recovers its balance, soaring smoothly again, along with music from the soundboard.

 It's a big, big world. It's easy to get lost in it...

I love that line in the lyrics. Sometimes I feel like that's what everyone's expecting. My world got very big, very fast, and based on a lot of sad examples from the past, a lot of people expect me to get lost in it. I'm always getting asked the same two questions: 'How did you get started?' and 'How do you stay grounded?'

Standing there in the XL Center, I can see the answers to both: I'm surrounded by super-smart, super-talented, extremely good people who love me and watch out for me every step of the way. They don't let me lose sight of where I came from or where I'm going. And they don't let me get away with any crap. The success I've achieved comes to me from God, through the people who love and support me, and I include my fans in that. Every single one of you lifts me a little bit higher.

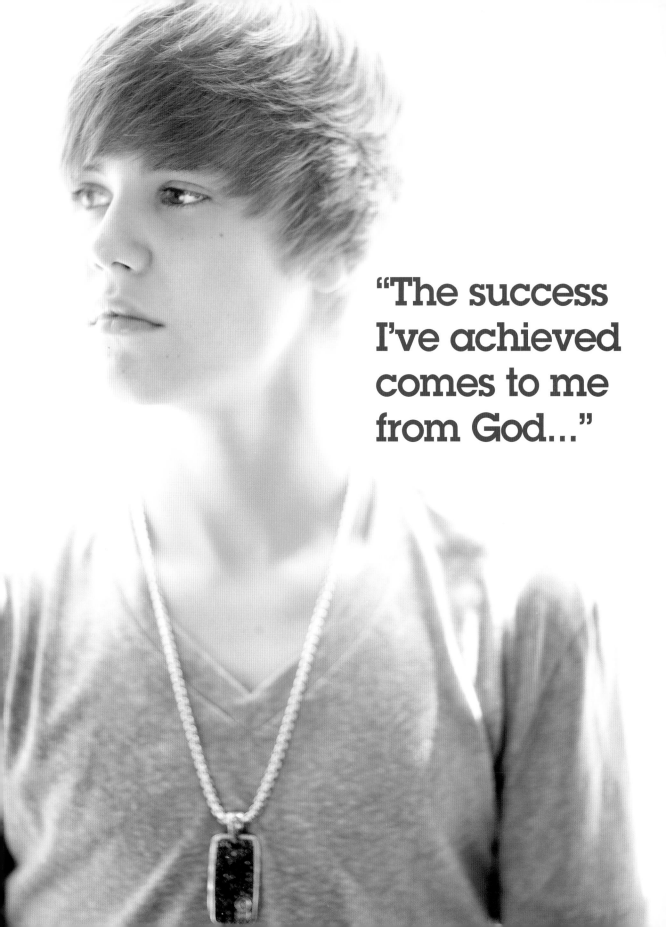

"The success I've achieved comes to me from God..."

"My world got very big, very fast, and based on a lot of sad examples from the past, a lot of people expect me to get lost in it"

...nowhere but up from here, my dear... Baby we can go nowhere but up. Tell me what we got to fear. We can take it to the sky, past the moon through the galaxy. As long as you're with me.

What a trip! Better than a Zamboni ride.

The reality of how really big this show is going to be hadn't fully sunk in until we got to the XL Center. The tour director, Tom Marzullo, Scooter and I came into it with all these huge ideas, and, once we started rehearsals, I was blown away at how amazing it's going to be. Huge rigs sailing through the air. A two-storey stage with ramps and platforms. Elevator rigs raise giant set pieces sky high and sink back down into the underworld. We've got fog machines, follow spots, my dancers and me flying fifteen feet above the floor – it's a huge super-cool production. I can't believe I'm here at the center of it all, and I feel a huge responsibility not to screw it up.

'It's a lot,' Grandpa says, as if he's reading my mind. 'It's... it's a lot. But you'll do okay, Justin. You just do what you do, and it'll work out fine.'

 ...we were underground, but we're on the surface now.

He has tears in his eyes. He does that a lot lately. He gets very emotional when he comes face to face with everything that's happened in my life. He's been known to burst into tears during TV interviews, and he's not at all hung up about that. This guy's a hockey-loving, elk-hunting, head-butting Canadian dude, tougher than anybody I know. I think that's why he's not afraid to show his feelings – how much he loves us, how proud he is of me and Mom and all his kids and grandkids – and that's why I'm not afraid to show my feelings either. (Well, most of the time. Within reason. You know what I'm saying.) I'm finally taller than my grandpa, but I'll always look up to him. He's there for me when I need him and has been since my earliest memories.

CHAPTER 2

A SECRET MUSICIAN

justinbieber Music is the universal language no matter the country we are born in or the color of our skin. Brings us all together

11:37 AM May 19th via web

The day I was born, 1 March 1994, Celine Dion was solid at #1 on the Billboard Hot 100 with 'The Power of Love'. Not a bad song to start your life on. My musical director Dan Kanter, whose guilty pleasure is Celine Dion, must have been really excited that day. It was all over the radio, so I probably heard her belting it out before I got my first look at the blue sky over Stratford, Ontario. My hometown is 2,450 miles northeast of Los Angeles, 530 miles northwest of New York City, 1,312 miles due north of Disney World, and totally on the other side of the world from Tokyo. But that day, people all over the planet were listening to Celine Dion and loving it.

I am a proud Canadian and I hope that comes through in everything I do. I love hockey, maple syrup and Caramilk bars. Canada is an awesome country in general, and Stratford is an excellent place to call home. The people are nice, but not easily impressed. I go back there to visit Grandpa and Grandma and my friends, Ryan and Chaz, as often as I can, and everybody treats me the same as always.

Stratford is a small town of about 30,500 people, named after Stratford-upon-Avon in England, which is the birthplace of William Shakespeare. So it makes sense that there's always a lot of comedy and drama going on and that our Stratford is the home of a huge Shakespeare festival – the biggest in North America. Every summer, about a million tourists come through to see the plays at the Avon Theatre, check out the local arts and crafts and poke around the town, which gets pretty quiet in the winter.

If you're looking at a map of North America, you'll see that Ontario is that little triangle of Canada that cuts down into the Great Lakes between New York and Michigan. Stratford is actually pretty close to the United States, halfway between Detroit and Buffalo, but, when I say I'm from Canada, some people think that means I came in from

"Everybody treats me the same as always"

the North Pole on a dog sled or something. Sometimes it does seem like winter lasts forever, but it's more because the kids are dying for the school year to be over. Summers are hot and muggy, but always a lot of fun. In the fall, the whole place is blazing with colors like you cannot believe. In the spring, it's incredibly beautiful. The snowmen keel over or get kicked down, the slush piles melt away, and the grass on the baseball diamond sort of struggles to wake up. The air is clean. Everything smells like wet pine trees.

"I'm a proud Canadian and I hope that comes through in everything I do"

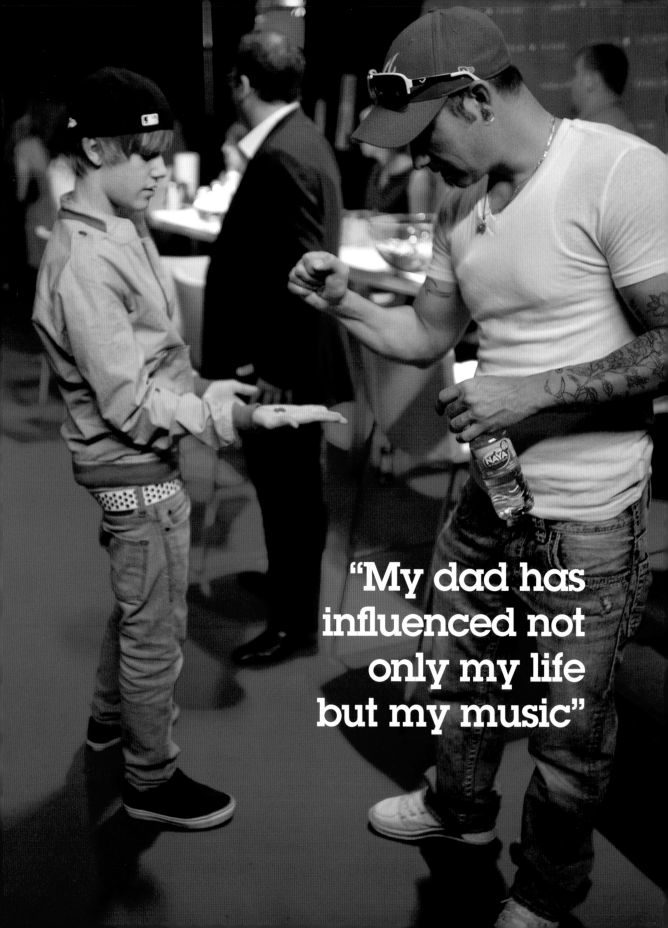

"My dad has influenced not only my life but my music"

My mom and dad were in their late teens when I was born. Not that much older than I am now. (And, yeah, that kinda freaks me out, so I don't dwell on it.) My dad, Jeremy Bieber, was basically a kid, doing his best to handle huge adult responsibilities. Lately, I've started to understand how hard that is. He and I have always had a great relationship, and as the story goes on you'll see how he's influenced not only my life but my music. I admire my mom so much for how she stepped up to meet all the challenges in her life.

My parents broke up when I was ten months old. Shortly afterwards, my dad started working on construction jobs out of town. Mom basically worked her butt off at whatever job she could get to keep a roof over our heads. We lived in public housing, and there were no luxuries at our little apartment, but it never occurred to me that we were poor. We had each other, which was everything we needed.

While Mom was working, I went to daycare, but I also spent a lot of time with my grandparents. I had a room at their house, and Grandma painted it blue and white with Toronto Maple Leafs stuff all over the walls. There was never any question about it: I was into hockey from day one, and the Maple Leafs were my favorite team.

Every summer, Grandpa and Grandma took us up to Star Lake, where they rented a cabin that belonged to the rod-and-gun club. Grandma's brothers and sisters would come, and Grandpa and I would go fishing with Grandma's dad. Being French Canadian,

"I'd really love to have a nice girlfriend"

he didn't speak English, and Grandpa didn't speak French, so there wasn't much conversation going on. But that's a cool thing I learned from fishing: sometimes you don't need conversation. Ha ha.

I spoke both French and English from the time I was little, so I could interpret when needed.

Grandpa would say, 'Ask him if he's hungry.'

And I'd go, *Avez-vous faim?*

Great-grandpa would nod enthusiastically. *Mais oui, j'ai très faim.*

But, for the most part, they both knew the important words. Fish, *poisson*. Boat, *bateau*. Water, *l'eau*. Thanks, *merci*. You're welcome, *pas de quoi*. I have to pee, *j'ai envie de faire pipi*. What else do you really need to know to get along?

'Fishing's not something you have to talk about. It just happens,' Grandpa says, and it seems to me that a lot of things in life are that way. I mean, think how nice it is when you can hang out with someone and not have to fill up the air with small talk. I hate being on a date where both people are working too hard to come up with stuff to say. You know it's working when you can just chill − listen to music, watch a movie or whatever − without feeling like you have to force the conversation. It should just be natural. When it's working, there's room in the air for both people to say things that matter. Scooter gave me the smartest dating advice you could ever give – to a guy or a girl – just listen. And that means *really* listen to what the other person is saying instead of using that time to come up with your next clever remark.

Anyway. Yeah. Quiet mornings out on the water. There's not much of that in my life any more. I'm going at light speed 24/7 – and I love it. I'm grateful for all the blessings and opportunities that have come my way. But I will say that when I was little, I longed for a 'normal' life with a 'normal' family, and there's no way that's ever going to happen now. There's a circus going on around me everywhere I go, which makes it hard on my family sometimes. I'd really love to have a nice girlfriend, but she'd have to put up with all that. You won't hear me complain about how my life is going, but I hope someday I'll be out on Star Lake with my own grandkid, reeling in brown trout and telling stories about how all of us would get together by the fire pit in the evening, everybody laughing and talking at once, the same way we did at Christmas dinner.

justinbieber no better feeling than coming back home and seeing your grandparents standing there waiting for u. no judgments pure love

8:24 PM Jun 13th via web

BIG FAMILY CHRISTMAS

Our tradition was always to gather at Grandpa and Grandma's house early in the afternoon. She'd have the tree up and decorated with all the usual ornaments dragged down from the attic. People would start showing up, and by dinner time there was quite a crowd gathered. And not just the usual grandparents, kids, grandkids. Our extended family is really – well, I guess 'extended' is a good word.

See, my mom's biological father died when she was a baby, so Grandpa is totally her dad, but technically he's her stepfather, who married Grandma when Mom was two, which is how my mom actually ended up with a brother and a stepbrother both named Chris, because Grandpa already had kids from a previous marriage. It would suck for her stepsiblings and their kids not to be with their dad/grandpa at Christmas, so Grandpa's ex-wife and her husband come with their kids, plus cousins on this side, and step-sibs on the other side, and after a while it's pretty complicated trying to keep track of which cousin belongs to whose aunt, or who's the stepson of the great-uncle, or the grandkid of the step-aunt – and you end up realizing it really doesn't make any difference.

We're a family.

We all have Christmas dinner, and I'm telling you, my grandma puts up an *awesome* Christmas dinner. Turkey and gravy. I wish I could have a trough of that stuff on my bus after the show. (We all work up an appetite during a performance.) It's the best. We all eat until we're about to roll over. Then we play this gift-exchange game with dice. Everybody shows up with a gift. If you're a girl, bring a gift for a girl; if you're a guy, bring a gift for a guy. That way there's the right number of each. You take turns rolling the dice, and, if you roll doubles, you grab a gift. If you roll doubles again, you get to grab somebody else's gift. There's always a lot of horsing around and teasing, but nobody actually gets mad because you don't know what's in the package anyway, so why would you care if your gift gets stolen? You get another turn, and the game keeps going until everybody has a gift. Then we all open our gifts and end up trading anyway.

That's how we are in my family. Every person gives what they have. If this particular gift isn't what you need, maybe that gift over there works for you, and, meanwhile, the first gift is exactly what somebody else needs. You can't always get what you want. But, if you're lucky, you get what you need. And I was lucky. Along with a lot of other blessings, I got my family — just the way they are. And now my extended family extends even wider to include Scooter, Carin, Kenny, Ryan and Dan and a lot of other people I'll tell you about a little later in this book.

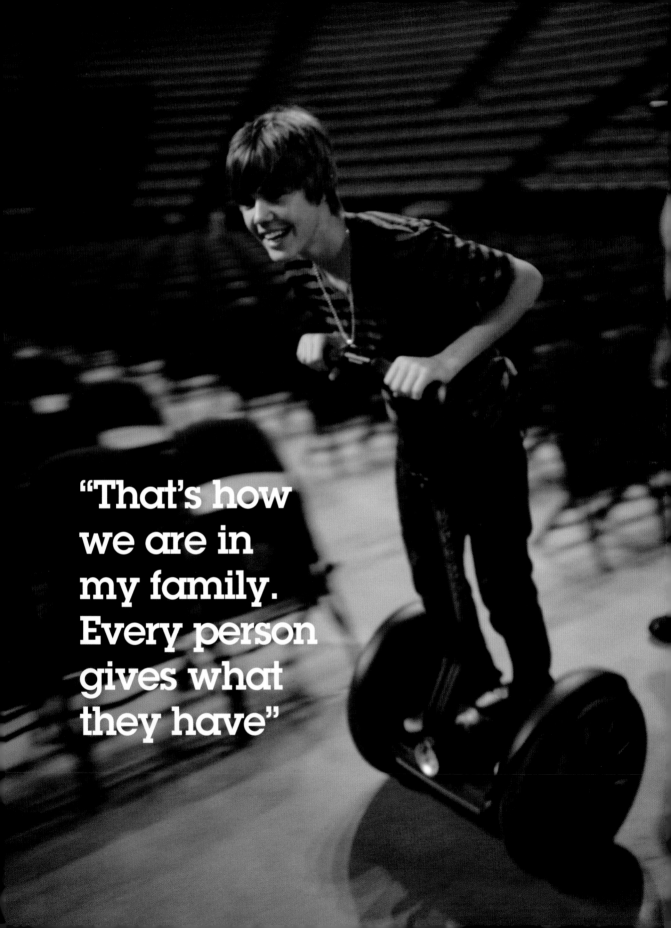

"That's how we are in my family. Every person gives what they have"

DOWN TO EARTH

I wrote the song 'Down to Earth' a few years ago, and I was really excited to record it for the *My World* album. It's a huge fan favorite. So many people feel where I'm coming from. It doesn't need any spectacular stage effects in the touring show; the best thing I can do is just sing it straight from my heart. I'm not afraid to show my emotions; if you love someone, you should tell them. If you think a girl is beautiful, you should say that. Usher says some songs work best when there's a sob in the singer's voice. You gotta let that deep feeling come through. And that's how I felt about this song. Sometimes the emotion of it is enough to bring tears to my eyes.

No one has a solid answer.
We're just walking in the dark.
And you can see the look on my face,
It just tears me apart . . .
So we fight through the hurt
And we cry and cry and cry and cry
And we live and we learn
And we try and try and try and try

"'Look for the good,' Grandpa says"

At the end of the day, families are what they are. If you feel like a freak because you don't have a normal family, I've got news for you: pretty much nobody does. In fact, I don't know if there's any such thing as a 'normal' family, and if there is, they'd probably be the most boring people ever. Or the scariest. Seriously, it would be creepy to even have dinner with the Perfect Family. The whole time you'd be thinking they can't be this perfect, they're probably holding the butcher's knife under the table ready to kill me, or they've got a mailman chained up in the basement or something. All families − even the ones that seem perfect on the outside − have their issues to some degree. What counts is how you handle it.

'Look for the good,' Grandpa says.

In our family, all the kids know they're loved, and, for the most part, everybody's able to just get over themselves and be cool. You just love and accept everybody as they are. You forgive others and hope that others will forgive you, because God forgives us all six hundred times a day, and he doesn't sit around busting heads about it.

 So it's up to you and it's up to me
That we meet in the middle
On our way back down to earth...

My dad was away at work a lot of the time, and, yeah, that sucked for me sometimes. It sucked for him, too. But in life you realize that the world's not perfect and if it had been up to us we'd have been together all of the time. And it sucked for my mom, because being a single parent is never easy, especially with a little prankster like me. There were times when my mind went to 'What if such and such?' or 'It could have been like da-da-da.'

But, as of right now, my life is working out pretty sweet and every morning I wake up grateful for the blessings that I have.

> **"I admire her so much for how she got her life together and made a life for me"**

Two of those blessings are my new baby brother, Jaxon, and my little sister, Jazmyn, who are my dad's children and are the cutest kids in the world. I would do anything for them.

Now I'm on the road, I won't be around as much as I wish I could be while they're growing up, but they'll always know I'm their big brother and I love them. I wouldn't trade them for all the what-ifs and could-have-beens in the world.

My mom has been upfront and honest with me about the choices she made when she was my age, some of which were not the best and made life difficult for her and her family. Before I was born, she started going to church, and that became super-important to her. She could see the kind of person and the kind of Mom she wanted to be.

After she had me, she had to work really hard all the time, but she never complained. She let me be myself, but she kept an eagle eye on me, stayed strong about discipline, and impressed on me the importance of doing the right thing and keeping God in my life. I admire her so much for how she learned from her mistakes, got her life together, and made a life for me.

STAR-CROSSED LOVERS

I was two years old in 1996 when The Cardigans had their monster hit 'Lovefool', the lead single from their *First Band on the Moon* album. It was featured in this crazy film adaptation of Shakespeare's *Romeo and Juliet*, which is also dope. Any guy can relate to Romeo, who's trying really hard to be cool in front of his crew, but he can't stop looking at all these beautiful girls all over Verona, and then he falls victim to one of the killer crushes of all time.

 My friends say I'm a fool to think that you're the one for me.
I guess I'm just a sucker for love . . .

That's me. Total sucker for love. That's not a bad thing. What kind of jerk doesn't want love? I bet 95% of sixteen-year-old guys would admit to thinking forty-five girl-related thoughts every three minutes. (The other 5% would be lying.) Everybody wants love, and there's something about that *Romeo and Juliet* theme – the star-crossed lovers who can't be together because of what other people have to say about it.

'It's universal,' says Dan Kanter (my lead guitarist, musical director – and possibly nicest guy in the world). 'It strikes a chord.'

Dan looks like a young version of Paul Simon and plays like – like – well, he plays like Dan Kanter. I can't even think of anything to compare it to. Except maybe a mix of Fergie and Jesus. He has a bachelor's degree in classical composition and analysis and is currently getting his master's degree in musicology.

'Not a performance degree,' he specifies. 'Music in society. I try not to think about theory when I'm on stage, but classical music taught me that art history was very linear, and now it's fragmented, and I really enjoy that.'

Okaaaaaay??? I'm not really sure what he's talking about but obviously Dan is pretty smart. I guess what he might be trying to say is music is part of all of our lives, that it's like a timeline. Looking back, I see this trail of music, a million great songs that came out of the radio and passed through my head over the years, and every once in a while one of them pops up in something I'm doing now, because it's all part of me.

Tom really took our vision on and designed a crazy cool opening for the touring show, and I don't want to give any of the surprises away, but I get to sort of emerge from the fog and slam into 'Love Me'. The show's opening makes me sound like a bad-ass.

"I get to sort of emerge from the fog and slam into 'Love Me'. The show's opening makes me sound like a bad-ass."

BEAT IT

Back in 1996, Mom says I was all about the beat. And I suppose that makes sense. Before anything else, you gotta have rhythm. She loved pop music and played the radio loud when we were in the car. At home, she'd crank her stereo listening to Boyz II Men or Michael Jackson. I'd wail on whatever was handy – pots and pans, plastic bowls, tables and chairs – with whatever else was handy. Like a spoon or the phone or my fists. She got me a little toy drum kit, probably to keep me from destroying the place, and

I hammered on that until people started noticing I was actually laying down a pretty sick beat.

My mom is an absolute sweetheart who has this vivacious, goofy personality, so there were always a lot of interesting, artsy people hanging around our place. I think artsy people who can't afford to go anywhere tend to hang out in the living room of the coolest person, playing guitars and talking about philosophy or whatever, and that's the living room I grew up in. (I guess I just also realized that with my mom being single, a lot of those guys were probably hitting on her, but again: freakout factor. Not gonna go there.)

At the church my mom went to, there was a lot of music during worship, and most of it was backed by a contemporary praise band. The people in the band were friends, and, while we were hanging out with them, sometimes the percussionist would let me play with the various noisemakers. When he saw that I wanted to play – not just play – he'd let me sit on his knee while he played on the drum kit, and, after a while, he handed me the sticks and let me have a go at it.

By the time I was four or five, I could climb up on the stool and play the kit all by myself, and, about that same time, I discovered I could get up on the piano bench and pound on that, too.

Much to everyone's surprise, it started sounding like actual music.

So here might be a good place to stop and say that if there's an annoying little kid in your life – a little brother or some kid you babysit for – who wants to make noise and pretend to play music, I hope you'll put up with him. Because, at some point, he won't be playing any more. He'll be *playing*. Kids have to be allowed to do things they're no good at. How else are they supposed to learn?

And, while you're at it, you have to let yourself do stuff you're not good at. Don't get hung up on what other people think about what you're doing. Dare to be a sucky skateboarder or a lousy video editor or a completely crappy golfer. If we do only the stuff we're good at, we never learn anything new. Think of all the great possibilities in life that pass by because we're too chicken to explore them and risk looking like a loser. Screw the haters who have nothing better to do than make fun of people who are brave enough to put themselves out there. Get out of your comfort zone and go for it. You never know unless you try.

'Nuff said. Back to when I was five.

I was actually getting to be pretty good on the drums, and not too heinous on the piano. Mom and one of her musician friends Nathan McKay, who my grandparents called 'the Lion King' because of his big, bushy beard, decided that I needed a real drum set of my very own. Nathan, aka 'the Lion King' and a bunch of his friends pulled together a little benefit event at a local bar, where they played music and collected donations to buy me my first real trap set with a kick drum, floor toms, snare, hi-hat and boom cymbal. I went crazy on it. Now Mom had to crank the stereo loud enough for me to play along.

"You have to let yourself do stuff you're not good at"

Some of the church band people were playing at the fair that summer, and they invited me to play drums with them, but I was so little that the emcee couldn't see me sitting there ready to play. He was like, 'Well, I see you guys brought a drum set, but where's the drummer?' I gave him a little tasty

lick – ba-dum-bum-chhh! – and he stretched to see me back there behind the cymbal boom. Then he goes to the audience, 'You won't believe this. No way! There's a little guy back there with his hat on backwards.'

I kept playing and getting better over the next couple of years. It got to be 2000, 2001, and you know what that means.

Beyoncé.

Destiny's Child blew up out of Houston and killed everybody with 'Survivor' and 'Bootylicious'. That same year, I heard Alicia Keys' 'Fallin'', and I still can't get enough of that song. Usher murdered 'U Remind Me'. Missy 'Misdemeanor' Elliot did that crazy cool video for 'Get Ur Freak On', and there was that insane remake of 'Lady Marmalade' by Christina Aguilera, Lil' Kim, Mya and Pink. Plus, we heard from Outkast, Nelly, Uncle Kracker, Mary J. Blige – all in all, it was a very good year for music.

FEELING THE MUSIC

When I was six, I started first grade at Jeanne Sauvé Catholic School in Stratford, but after school I was banging on those drums and getting my musical education on the radio. I was also figuring things out on the piano. I couldn't read music (I was just beginning to read books), and Mom couldn't afford lessons for me, but I knew what I wanted the music to sound like. I could feel it when the chords and melody didn't fit together, the same way you can feel it when your shoes are on the wrong feet. I just kept poking and experimenting until it fit the way I wanted it to. When I listened to music in church, I could feel those harmonies hanging in the air like humidity. It wasn't an issue of learning it exactly: it was more as if the music soaked in through my skin. I don't know how else to explain it.

As soon as I was big enough to get my arms around a guitar, I started figuring that out, too. You have to build up strength in your hands, and, until you build calluses on your fingertips, it feels like razor blades. That probably discourages a lot of people. They start out thinking, 'Hey, playing guitar would be fun. And it looks pretty easy.' After thirty minutes or so, they're like, 'Ow! This really hurts.' And they forget about how much fun it was supposed to be and give up.

The thing is, if you keep on it, you get used to it pretty fast, and then you just keep plugging away at it while you're watching TV or waiting for supper. Or sitting in your room because you're

"Mom couldn't afford lessons for me, but I knew what I wanted the music to sound like... it soaked in through my skin"

grounded for mouthing off. But we don't need to go into that. The point is, I played guitar because it was fun, and, by the time I was eight or nine, I was alright.

The best times were when my dad was one of the people hanging out playing guitar in our living room. He wasn't a big fan of pop music. He was more into classic rock and heavy metal. He taught me some stuff like 'Knockin' on Heaven's Door' and a few other Dylan songs, turned me onto Aerosmith, Metallica, and Guns N' Roses, which got me listening to (and showing respect for) the legends like Jimi Hendrix and Eddie Van Halen. My dad taught me how to play 'Smoke on the Water' by Deep Purple, and I still remember it. (You should hear Dan Kanter and me kill that thing.)

To play metal or even the 1980s hair band stuff like Journey and Twisted Sister, you've gotta know the so-called power chords, and Dad taught me a few tricks there, too. He showed me how to play barré chords, which is when you lay your index finger flat across all the strings at once, which moves the chords up a little on the neck of the guitar. You're essentially playing the same chords, but changing the key, so you can play the song in whatever range fits your voice. If you know the basic form of five or six barré chords, you can play pretty much any song in the universe. Grab the lyrics off the Web, listen to the changes and progressions five or six times, and there you go. You're Green Day. In your room, that is.

ROCKIN' ROBIN

I was Metallica and Matchbox 20 in my room at night, but at school by day I was just me. Nobody at school knew anything about this part of my life. I was a hockey kid like all my friends, and I liked it that way. I was already a little odd because Jeanne Sauvé Catholic School was a French immersion school. It's exactly what it sounds like. You're immersed in French. They don't speak English at all. The idea is that you learn to speak French while you're learning to add and subtract and all the other things you'd be learning at a regular school.

I had a lot of friends at my French school, but, when I was seven or eight, I started playing house league hockey with a bunch of guys who went to regular English-speaking public school. I didn't need them to think I was a music geek in addition to being a French geek. (Of course, now I'm really glad that I speak French, because, let's face it, girls dig it when a guy speaks French. They call it the language of love, and that ain't no coincidence. Plus, I love my French fans! *Très jolie!*)

My best friends – from that day to this – were my hockey mates, especially Chaz Somers and Ryan Butler, and, man, did we have fun back then!

We weren't bad kids at all, but we were kinda out of control at times. We'd go down in the basement at Grandpa and Grandma's

house to watch TV and end up playing kickball with the couch pillows or battling a soccer ball back and forth or practically strangling each other with professional wrestling moves. We never destroyed anything major, but there were a few small casualties. A couple of lamps were sacrificed. And, among Grandpa's hunting trophies, there's a stuffed fox that mysteriously ended up missing a leg.

'You guys know anything about this?' he asked.

We all looked at him as innocent as could be. 'No. No, sir. That wasn't us.'

Once we sneaked out and went bike-riding at two o'clock in the morning, and the cops picked us up and took us home. My mom came unglued about that, and I was grounded for a few weeks, but that gave me time to work on my barré chords and a couple good guitar riffs and learn some new songs.

We call Ryan 'Butsy' which probably isn't Ryan's favorite thing, but sorry, dude, if you got 'butt' in your name, how are people not going to jump on that? Butts are funny to nine-year-olds. In fact, butts are funny to everybody. There's some stuff that's beyond your control, like your name. Other stuff — such as volunteering the information that you sometimes stand in front of the bathroom mirror pretending to be Michael Jackson and singing 'Rockin' Robin' into a blow-dryer — that's something you can and probably should keep to yourself.

Not that I ever did that…much.

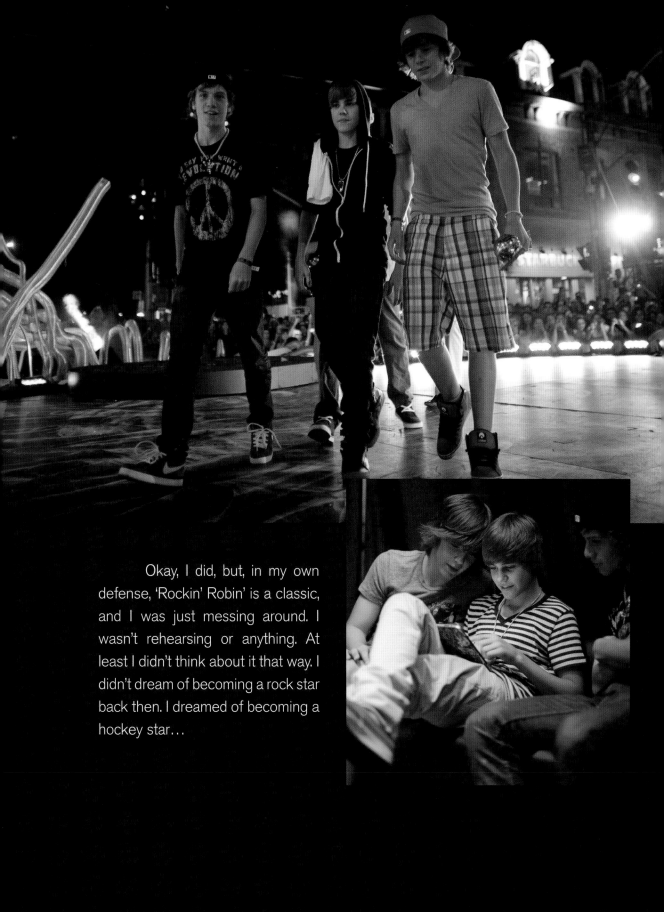

Okay, I did, but, in my own defense, 'Rockin' Robin' is a classic, and I was just messing around. I wasn't rehearsing or anything. At least I didn't think about it that way. I didn't dream of becoming a rock star back then. I dreamed of becoming a hockey star…

CHAPTER 3

THE STRATFORD STAR

J amaica Craft, our amazing choreographer, got her start out on the street. Never took formal dance lessons. She just danced the way she felt like dancing, and people were into it. Some pretty big people. She started dancing professionally about ten years ago, and, a few years later, stars started coming to her, asking, 'Can you make up this breakdown for me?' Genius. Everything Jamaica does looks like dancing. Even when she's just standing around talking, her crazy lime-green fingernails look like they're dancing. If you ask her how she does it, she shrugs and says, 'Just listen to the record. It'll tell you what to do.'

The day I met Jamaica, she fractured her foot. She wasn't even sure how it happened. She was literally just standing there having a conversation with Scooter and, wham, she was out for twelve weeks. Standing on the set of the touring show, she preps me to rehearse the flying trick (sorry to spoil the surprise) along with Nick and Mike, two of the backup dancers.

'Dancers are athletes,' Jamaica reminds us. 'We don't get pampered like athletes. You ain't got no masseuse down in here. You won't be getting any spa treatment after the show. But we can get hurt like athletes get hurt. You've got to take care of yourselves. Take care of each other.'

Fully aware of that, we've been rehearsing this show twelve hours a day. There are a lot of safety precautions we have to take. The choreography involves my flipping upside down in a harness

"A lot of hard work goes with performing"

about thirty feet in the air. I've been trying to get comfortable with both the dance choreography and the staging – where to be on the stage, and what I'm doing when I get to that part of the stage. A lot of hard work goes with performing. My set is seventy-five minutes long, and it's not easy. I work hard on endurance training, but I'm still hella tired by the end of the show. I go everywhere in a matter of seventy-five minutes. Never a dull moment. We rehearse every transition so the audience is never bored for one second. There are more than five-hundred people working to make sure the show goes perfect.

Nick, Mike and I get into our flying harnesses. Jamaica smacks each one of us on the butt and says, 'Kill it.' The music comes up on the sound board. I'm on my way up, up, up until I'm only about ten feet below the follow-spot rigs. High enough that I don't want to look down. Something doesn't feel right. When I go to do the flip, the harness isn't where it's supposed to be.

'Hey, you guys? Hey! Somebody?'

The music's too loud. No one can hear me.

'Guys! Something's messed up here!'

Nick and Mike are doing their thing, feet in the air, not even looking at me. I make a broad gesture, hoping somebody will get the idea that it means Down! Now! The music stops.

'Everything okay up there?' says Jamaica.

'No. I am about to die. Get me down.'

My heart's still pounding after my feet are on the floor. Holy crap! That sucked a little. That could have ended badly. Mom is hustling across the arena with a very Mom-mode look on her face.

'What's wrong? Was there a malfunction with the safety harness?'

'He's okay,' Jamaica calls. She puts her hand on the back of my neck. 'You're okay. It was hooked up solid. You weren't going to fall. Just part of it got tangled on the mike pack, so it was sitting kind of not quite right.'

'Okay.' I want to be cool, but I tell her I need to step off and take five.

'We can be fine with that,' she says calmly, unhooking the harness. 'Dance is supposed to get your pulse racing, but–'

'Not like that.'

'No. Not like that. But you're okay.'

'Geez,' I mumble as I walk off stage. 'I used to think hockey was dangerous.'

MY FAVORITE GIRL

Nothing ever got my pulse racing (in a good way) like hockey. Well, nothing except Beyoncé, but that wasn't until I was twelve or so. Then, all of a sudden, it was like I opened my eyes one day and noticed that the world is full of beautiful girls, and I've had a hard time thinking about anything else ever since.

When I was twelve, I left French immersion school and went over to Northwestern, a public middle school in Stratford. Chaz and Ryan and I had all moved up from the house hockey league to the travel league, and Grandpa used to go with me on the bus to the away games. We'd get to the game and play our hearts out, and on the way home we'd either be wired from winning and create more havoc than ever, or we'd be weary and discouraged from getting our butts kicked and end up getting into fights.

"One day I noticed the world was full of beautiful girls"

All the players would sit at the back of the bus, and all the parents would sit up front, not wanting to know what was going on back there. Of course, what was going on was a lot of guy talk. We were all completely fascinated with girls, freaked out about the way we were changing, and, more importantly, freaked out

about the way the girls were changing, and of course, we were all clueless idiots who didn't know what to do with any of that.

I had a great advantage in that I had lived in girl world all my life. My mom and I had talked about stuff pretty openly, so maybe I understood a little bit more than the average guy about how girls work. I wasn't afraid to talk to girls, hang out with girls, look at girls and well, you know, flirt with girls – but I also had an idea of when not to talk to girls, hang out with girls, look at girls and flirt with girls.

Some guys ended up hurting a girl's feelings or making her mad, because they were working too hard to look cool. Not me. My mom had drummed into my head the difference between confident and cocky. I tried hard to stay on the confident side, and I wasn't always successful. Sometimes, I probably came off as cocky, but I tried to balance that by actually being a nice guy. A certain amount of success with the opposite sex comes down to the simple concept: don't be a jerk. You don't have to work hard at pretending you care about a girl's feelings if you actually do care – not just about girls, but about people in general.

"A certain amount of success with the opposite sex comes down to the simple concept: don't be a jerk"

In the video for 'One Less Lonely Girl' – which was a lot of fun to make, because they cast this gorgeous sixteen-year-old girl opposite me – the storyline is that this girl drops something at the Laundromat (don't get excited, it's just a scarf), and I send her on a treasure hunt to get it back. Somebody called it 'the musical equivalent of a chick flick' and I didn't immediately get that they meant it as an insult. They dissed this part where there are some puppies at a pet shop, and I was, like, 'What? Who doesn't like puppies? And, more important, who thinks pretending to not like puppies will make them more attractive to girls?' They also thought the lyrics were corny.

I'm gonna put you first.
I'll show you what you're worth...

I'm definitely open to suggestions. Maybe something like:

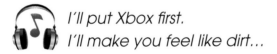
I'll put Xbox first.
I'll make you feel like dirt...

Yeah, that makes a lot of sense: I'm the lame one, and what really turns a girl on is a puppy hater who doesn't care about her feelings. Maybe if I get with that program I could someday achieve that critic's level of success with the ladies. Oh wait, I'm not a bitter old man.

Let's continue...

"I could move faster and play smarter"

WANNA BE STARTIN' SOMETHING

Back in middle school, most girls in my class were taller than I was. The last thing I wanted to do was give them another reason not to go out with me, so it seemed like a good idea to just be a nice guy. I also figured I'd keep the music thing on the down-low and stick with something I knew I could look cool doing – playing sports.

Guys don't engage in nearly as much drama as girls do at that age, but, when we do, look out. Heads get punched. Some people need to feel big, and the only way they can is to pick on somebody who's smaller. Unfortunately for the bullies, my dad was a former professional fighter who used to take me to his training sessions. I quickly got a reputation as someone not to be bullied even though some kids still tried. I think I learned from an early age that although I was smaller, I shouldn't pay attention to my size or let it stop me from going for something I knew I could achieve. I had nothing to prove to those guys, just as I have nothing to prove to the haters who try to tear me down now. I'm not a fighter by nature, but, if I believe in something, I stand up for it. If somebody talked trash about my friends or my mom, I'd let them know that was not cool. If somebody shoved me, I shoved back harder.

One time, an epic fight got organized off the school grounds. I don't remember what it was about or how I got sucked into it, but a bunch of people were involved and a bunch more were taking pictures and videos of it with their cellphones. Somebody posted their video on YouTube, for whatever reason. I guess it never occurred to them that teachers would see it. That's the thing about YouTube. You never know who's out there. That can be a good thing or a not good thing, depending on the situation.

Anyway, nobody got seriously hurt, but there were a lot of scrapes and bruises, and the video made it look like something out of Mortal Kombat, which we all thought was pretty awesome until school officials got POed about it and started busting people who couldn't sit there and deny that they were part of it, because, well, there they were on camera. (Apply that lesson to your own circumstances in any way you find helpful.)

Canadians are a scrappy bunch in general, but I was never a big fighter. My dad always said he did enough fighting in his day for both of us. I preferred to compete on the basketball court or slice and dice them with my hockey skills. I was a lot smaller than most of the guys in the hockey league, and I definitely wasn't playing Forward on the basketball team, but none of them could keep up with me. I knew I'd never be as tall as they were, but I could move faster and play smarter. I would try to skate circles around them or steal the basketball right out from under them.

That's another thing Grandpa always told me that you can probably apply to your own life: 'Make the most of what you've got.'

Anyway, I tried to steer clear when anything uncool went down at school. I was getting into enough trouble on my own. Nothing major. Class clown stuff mostly. Outside, I'd be showing off on my skateboard, kicking a soccer ball around, or just stirring things up with Chaz and Ryan, and it was hard to turn that off inside the building. I'm one of those people who have a lot of energy. If I got in trouble at school, it was never for being mean. It was for laughing. Or making someone else laugh. Or dancing in the hallway or drumming on my desk or humming in the library. Basically, I got in trouble for being myself, and that didn't seem fair to me.

"Grandpa always told me...make the most of what you've got"

One time I was sent to the Principal for clowning around. I walked down the hall toward the office, but then I just kept on walking. So long, suckers. I went out the door, up the street, and across town, all the way to my grandparents' house, thinking I'd find some sympathy there. Not a chance. Grandpa was very surprised and not very happy when he found me with my feet up in the living room, watching TV. He put me in the car and took me back to school, where I had

"I'm not a fighter by nature, but, if I believe in something, I stand up for it"

to go in and face the Principal, who wanted to know where I'd been for the last hour and a half when I was supposed to be at school. By the time Mom got home from work that afternoon, they'd called her and told her all about it, which gave her plenty of time to work up a good wrath and think of a bunch of harsh things to say. Grounded again. I sat in my room, busting on those barré chords for a couple more weeks.

'DUDE, YOU'RE PRETTY GOOD'

Nobody in my family lets me off the hook if I'm in the wrong, but they're always on my side when I do the right thing. I don't remember playing a basketball game when there wasn't somebody who loved me in the stands. My memories of hockey games, as a player and a fan, will always be about how my grandpa shared that with me. My family and best buds were always there for me, so I knew I'd have at least a few friendly faces in the audience when I decided to enter a local talent competition hosted by the Stratford Youth Centre in January 2007.

The few people who'd heard me do music kept telling me, 'Dude, you're pretty good. You should try out for *American Idol.*' But you had to be sixteen for that – as old as you had to be for a driver's license. To a twelve-year-old kid, that seemed like a million years away, so I never thought that much about it. The Stratford Star competition was basically the same idea on a smaller scale: all kids, aged twelve to eighteen, in a series of elimination rounds. The cost was two dollars at the door. Instead of Randy, Simon and Paula, we had some local folks who were involved in the community music scene, directing the church choir or teaching at the high school or whatever, and, instead

"I wasn't nervous about performing... my mom was more nervous than I was"

of Ryan Seacrest, we had this really nice girl who organized the summer music programs. The grand prize was a microphone you could use to record on your computer, plus a couple of hours at a local recording studio.

I thought that would be a fun prize, but I was more into the idea of getting up in front of people and doing music just to see how it felt. I wasn't nervous about performing, because I was used to playing basketball and hockey in front of crowds much bigger than this. But this was going to be the first time I'd ever sang publicly. Anyway, what's to be afraid of? The few people who knew me were people who loved me, and the rest were strangers, so if I didn't do well it wasn't like I'd ever have to see them again. My mom was more nervous that I was, I think, even though the understanding was that this was just for fun. She helped me

figure out what to wear and made sure I had the background track and all that.

For the first round I wore a huge brown sweater and jeans, and I did Matchbox 20's '3 AM'. The girl introduced me, and there was a little bit of polite applause when I went up on stage. I said, 'Hey, everybody' and tried to get them clapping on the intro. Mom and Grandma were out there with smiles a mile wide, clapping away, but most of the crowd just sat there looking bored.

Okay . . . so I started singing.

Then they perked up a little. I saw some heads nod, like people were thinking, 'Hey, this little dude's not bad!' By the end, they were surprised that this kid in the too-big sweater could actually sing pretty well, and the applause was a little more enthusiastic. This was the first time I heard an audience actually cheer for me on stage, and it felt pretty good. I made it through to the next round.

I thought I'd dress up a little for the next performance. Mom ironed a blue dress shirt for me and helped me do the knot on a sharp blue necktie, which was made for a grown man, so it was longer than I was tall. I decided to sing Alicia Keys' 'Fallin'" – which was my jam in the shower. When I came out, people remembered me from the week before. They were even more surprised and cheered even louder. That didn't just feel good. That felt kind of… thrilling.

By the time I got to the next round, I'd settled into the idea that I should just be myself, so I wore my regular school clothes and a baseball cap. I decided to do the Aretha Franklin arrangement on 'Respect'. By now people knew who I was. The girl doing the emcee duties said, 'Let's show Justin Bieber some respect.' And there was a burst of loud, shrill screaming from the back of the room.

A group of girls. Beautiful girls. Screaming. For me.

Holy crap!

I got up there and sang my little eighth-grade butt off, thinking this was possibly the greatest moment of my entire life – of anyone's life – better than hockey, better than *Star Wars*, better than Grandma's turkey and gravy. A few people up front looked like they were sitting on something pointy, but those girls in the back were into the number, swaying and clapping. I was feeding off the energy and it felt great, and, when I got to the instrumental break, I hammed it up, playing air sax. I got so big with it, I dropped the mike, which made a loud thunk on the stage – but no problem – I grabbed it up just in time to plow into the next verse.

I brought it home with a wild blues run (I hope Aretha would have been proud), and there was big, appreciative applause, plus another shrill scream from those girls, so I gave it the classic Michael Jordan fist pump. The older contestants had been taking voice lessons for years and they were really good, but – wow! Girls were screaming for me.

I made it all the way to the last round of the competition, even though I was one of the youngest contestants and the other finalists were the oldest. The night of the final, after everyone had performed, one of the judges brought the three finalists up on stage. First a beautiful blonde who was tall and had all kinds of vocal training and sang great. Then a beautiful brunette who was even taller and more trained and sang even better. And then me. The twelve-year-old kid in baggy pants. But being surrounded by beautiful girls, win or lose, I wasn't complaining. I was feeling really good about how it went, but not

"I just got up there and sang my eighth-grade butt off"

Bieber
Fever

Savannah

Diana

"But being surrounded by
beautiful girls, win or lose,
I wasn't complaining"

justinbieber i hear everyday how many of you have met thru this, and how this all started. music brings people together and that is what i am proudest of

7:17 PM Jun 17th via web

cocky at all. I didn't assume I'd win, but I really, really, really wanted to. I hooked my thumbs in my pockets, trying to look like 'Hey, it's cool. Whatever.' But inside I was praying for that judge to say my name.

'I want to tell you that you're all winners,' she said.

Yeah. Awesome. Please, say my name now.

'It takes so much to get up on stage and showcase a talent like that. Music is important, so keep singing no matter what.'

Okay. Got it. Please, say my name. Please, say my name. Please, say my—

'Our Stratford Star winner this year is…'

She said someone else's name.

The crowd cheered. A little chunk of my heart fell out and rolled under the piano.

I came in third out of, um … how many was it again? Let me see, I believe it was … three. The only person they announced at the time was the winner, and for a long time I was under the

"The guys on the tour say I am a perfectionist"

impression I'd come in second, which was slightly less humiliating. But no. After my first record blew up, somebody from the competition told a reporter that I was actually third. She was quoted as saying, 'He was definitely up for the challenge, and he had the charisma. He just didn't have the experience. We thought, give him a couple years with voice training.'

Obviously, I'm pretty happy with the way things eventually worked out, but I was seriously crushed at the time. I just couldn't understand it. I'd felt so totally high on it – had this awesome experience – and then I lost? I won't even pretend I didn't care. I wanted to win. I mean, if you don't care about winning the competition, why show up? I know that sounds harsh but I just love competition so much that I'm sometimes very hard on myself. The guys on the tour say I'm a perfectionist. But I was old enough to know that you have to be prepared to be gracious, win or lose. Even at the time, I clapped. I smiled. I shook the winner's hand. I thanked the judges. Mom and Grandpa and Grandma were proud of the way I conducted myself. That's something you learn playing sports. You want to win. You play your heart out. If it goes your way – joy! Winning feels great. If you lose, that sucks, and you have every right to feel bad, but you have to suck it up, be gracious, and go down the line, slapping hands with the other team, saying,

'Good game, good game, good game . . .'

So shout out to those two girls who beat me in Stratford Star. Good game, ladies!

While we were working up this touring show, Dan Kanter said, 'I see a song from an aerial view. The intro, the verse, the chorus. And then I look at a show from the aerial view. The set list, the climax of a guitar solo. Writing a set list is an art. Before I go to concerts, I never look online. I want to go in and everything is a surprise. It's too bad that, with YouTube, the fans are going to know so much in advance. They're still going to freak out and think it's great, but I wish it was a full reveal.'

On stage, we don't want any surprises. We want everything to play out perfect, just the way we planned. In life, you get the full reveal. It's all a surprise. And that makes it a lot more interesting, even though some of the surprises suck. In the Bible it says 'everything works together for good' if you love God, but there are times when it does not feel that way at all. Times when you're like, 'Yo, God! This is messed up. Could you pay some attention down here?' Maybe faith is the ability to chill and trust that somebody up there got the set list right. Maybe when you're cool with whatever comes your way, the reveal eventually happens, and even the bad moments can turn around to bless you.

Mom and Grandpa and Grandma took me to Scoopers Ice Cream after I lost the Stratford Star competition.

Grandpa told me, 'You can lose without feeling like a loser. If you take the experience and learn from it, you're still coming out ahead of where you were before.'

'We're so proud of you,' said Grandma. 'And remember, you did it for fun, and it was fun, right? You had fun, didn't you?'

'Yeah . . .' I had to admit it. I had a ton of fun. It was actually kind of an incredibly fun experience, and I could definitely see myself doing that again. Or doing some other competition. Maybe even *American Idol* someday. In a thousand years. When I'd have a driver's license. And probably a beard like Nathan, that Lion King dude...'Plus, you're invited to sing for the autism benefit,' said Mom. 'Are you excited about that?'

'Yeah. Kind of. I will be when it gets closer to the time to do it,' I said, trying not to sound too destroyed.

Mom gave me a good hug. 'You did great, Justin. I wish everyone could have been there – the whole family and all our friends at church. But I got some great videos. I'm going to put them up on YouTube so everyone can all see how amazing you did.'

CHAPTER 4

YouTube: MY FIRST MILLION

Underneath the stage, it's like a whole city of steel beams, cables, equipment, rolling storage units and canvas curtains. Part of the stage floor drops down and elevators rise up with me onboard for a dramatic entrance, and coming down from the sides are ramps the dance crew and I use to exit. They lead to a narrow alley that's curtained off and lit with flood lamps. All the costume changes are hanging on racks, carefully arranged in order of who belongs to which pair of pants and when in the show everything is needed.

After a lunch break and some ping-pong with the crew we charge into a second run-through of the show. The morning run-through was for working out the last few bugs in the technical stuff. No screw-ups this time. We're cruising through the whole thing without stopping.

Ryan Good, my stylist and road dog, keeps everything rocking right along. When I come off stage, he helps me do a quick change into the next get-up. It's pretty hectic — there's me and the whole dance crew and we're all working pretty hard. When we strip off our sweaty shirts and shoes, it smells like that sweaty old guy from the YMCA. You guys know what I'm talking about.

In addition to those costume changes, we have to work out the timing between one song and the next, and how the talking will fit with the video effects, which means I have to say something, but it changes from one show to the next. So, during

the run-through, I'm just supposed to say whatever comes into my head, and usually what comes into my head is a bunch of goofing off and teasing people.

'How y'all doing out there tonight? Oh, Ryan, you are looking good today. Was it Garnier Fructis you used last night?'

Somewhere in the dark arena, a voice yells, 'Video rolling for forty-five…forty…'

'Man you've got some golden locks. AW C'MON!'

There's laughter from underneath the stage and heckling from roadies and catering people wandering around. I suppose I could practice what I'm actually going to say, but I don't want it to come out sounding phony. I'd rather just come out and look at the real faces of the real people and talk to them. As carefully as we nail down everything else, that connection has to stay unrehearsed and in the moment. I don't know who's going to be out there or what's going to happen, but I know it has to be personal, and it doesn't scare me to leave it wide open.

That's another question I get asked all the time: 'Do you get nervous?'

The truth is: I don't. I don't mean for that to come off as cocky. I just don't see what's to be afraid of. It's not that I never make mistakes. Are you kidding? Mistakes happen all the time. But that's life. You pick it up and keep going. My spleen isn't going to explode if I play the wrong guitar chord or fluff the occasional song lyric. I'm kind of a perfectionist. I work hard to get it right, but part of that is being able to roll with the unexpected. I know someone who was busking in the park and a bird pooped on her head in the middle of 'Amazing Grace'. That's showbiz.

For those of you who don't know what busking is, that's when you play music for donations on the street, in a park, on the subway, or, in my case, on the front steps of the Avon Theatre…

SINGING ON THE SIDEWALK

I wanted to go golfing with my friends one day, but I didn't have any money. After the Stratford Star competition, I was excited about the idea of playing music for people, so I decided to give busking a shot. During tourist season, the Stratford Shakespeare Festival was going on, and people came from far and wide to see those plays. Buses would pull up in front of the theatre, and about a hundred people would get out and mill around before they went off to shop or check out the local cafés and art galleries.

So this was a perfect place. Lots of pedestrians. And shade, if I went there at the right time of day. I knew all the words to a

lot of songs and I didn't need backup tracks. I could accompany myself on the guitar. Mom wasn't sure what people were going to be like, so she didn't want me sitting there by myself. I tried to tell her it would be fine and I'd be home by dark, but she insisted on having Grandpa sit in his car across the street.

The first time I parked myself on the steps, I set my open guitar case in front of me, hoping people would be nice and I'd come up with twenty bucks or so. After just a couple hours, I had almost $200. I felt like I'd discovered a gold mine. When I got home and shared this discovery with Mom, she was completely blown away and immediately started talking about responsibility and a college account and that sort of thing. I had another idea.

'Mom, we could go to Disney World.'

She thought about the math for a minute and said, 'We seriously could. At this rate, even if you put a good share into savings, you'd have enough for plane tickets by the end of summer.'

It was a plan. Mom and I had never gone anywhere on vacation except up to the rod-and-gun club cabin at Star Lake with Grandpa and Grandma. Disney World had always seemed about as possible as winning the lottery. The realization that I could make it happen just by playing music – doing something I'd been doing for years just for fun – was pretty cool. Mom was satisfied the people were going to be nice, but now she was worried about my sitting there with all that cash, so she and Grandpa took turns keeping an eye on me from across the street.

Busking was a blast. People were very kind and appreciative. Almost everybody threw me at least a buck or two and had something nice to say. At the end of one day, there was a note in my guitar case. I don't remember exactly what it said, but it was something to the effect of 'You're cute! Call me! Love, Tiffany.' And a phone number.

Chaz and Ryan were so like, 'Whuuuut? No way!'

Way.

It's hard to imagine improving on the situation, but this was getting ridiculously awesome. Disney World… plus girls. Busking was a pretty sweet gig!

"Disney World had always seemed about as possible as winning the lottery"

The acoustics were great at that location, and on clear, calm days people told me they could hear me all the way down the street. Buses came and went, bringing all sorts of people. Ladies with big hats and giant bags, Japanese schoolgirls in plaid uniforms, Boy Scout troops and baseball teams, elderly couples out for a stroll. Tour groups would get dropped off on the corner so they could shop for souvenirs, and some of them would still be

"I was twelve... I wanted to start dating"

standing there when the bus came back.

Thanks to the musical influences of Mom and Dad, I had a nice repertoire that included something for everybody. Anything from R&B and pop standards to country and Christian music, and even a little heavy metal. Which isn't very heavy when it's just a kid and his guitar, I guess, but – you know. Mini metal. It works.

One song that consistently wrecked people to tears and brought in a lot of donations was 'Sarah Beth', a Rascal Flatts song about a girl with cancer. Look up that video on YouTube and try to watch it without getting choked up. I dare you. 'Sarah Beth' wrecks everybody. I don't care if you're one of those gnarly, bearded Bering Strait crab fishermen on *Deadliest Catch*. You're crying by the end of that song.

People who ran the shops close to the theater loved me because customers lingered longer when I was playing. If it was up to them, I'd have been out there every day from open to close of business, but it was summertime and I was twelve. I wanted to hang out with my friends. And I wanted to start dating. I was feeling pretty flush in the financial department, more than ready to step up, be a gentleman, show a lady a good time.

VIRAL VIDEO

My first date has been sort of mythologized as 'Bieber's Dating Disaster'. I took her to King's, a buffet restaurant. Yes, I wore a white shirt. Yes, I got spaghetti. No, this was not the brightest idea. But it wasn't a big trauma, though. This girl was a friend, and she's pretty cool. We laughed about it and, all things considered, while it wasn't one of my smoothest dating experiences, it gave us both a funny story to tell and it was a good starter date for me. I was a lot more nervous about that date than I ever was about performing on stage, but, once it was over with, I was comfortable with the idea of going out with other girls and just having fun. Seriously, if the worst thing that ever happened to a person on a date was getting a stain on your shirt . . . quit cryin'. That's nothing.

A lot of the tourists out in front of the Stratford Theatre were armed with video cameras, not surprisingly, and, pretty soon, a few videos of me busking showed up on YouTube. When I was searching around for them, I happened to click on one of Mom's videos from the Stratford Star.

'Geez, Mom, how many times did you and Grandma look at this video?' I said. 'There's like . . . whoa . . .'

The counter showed dozens of comments:

He's so cute!

OMG! I love Justin

Great Job! Adorable Kid!

Shut up, dork

You shut up! Don't mind the haterz, Justin.
UR SEXY!

Crazy. The busking videos had racked up hundreds of hits as well, with a similar supply of comments. As summer went on, hundreds turned to thousands. Mom started getting weird calls from people we didn't know.

'Does Justin have an agent?'

'I'd like to talk to you about being Justin's manager.'

We didn't get all excited about this, because Mom assumed that these people were con men – or worse. She got an email from a producer for the TV show *Maury* (which used to be called *The Maury Povich Show*), but I didn't even know what his show was about.

'I think they have all kinds of crackpots on that show,' Grandma said. 'Or they have people on and do paternity tests to determine who's a baby's father.'

Yikes! We definitely weren't interested in *that* one.

THE PHONE CALL OF A LIFETIME

One day, she got a call from the school district. A guy named Scooter Braun had called them looking for this kid from Stratford.

'I'm very skeptical of anyone in the music industry,' said Mom. 'I wish they'd leave him alone.'

They gave her Scooter's phone number, but she didn't call him back. So Scooter began calling around to people in the area, trying to find us. He was so persistent that my mom agreed to call him back from a blocked number to hear him out.

'Please, listen to me for just a minute, Pattie,' Scooter said. 'And then, if you don't want to hear from me again, you won't have to. I just want to say I see something really special in your son. And I see a lot of myself in him, except when I was that age I had no talent. I think I can help him.'

The fact that Mom didn't immediately hang up got me thinking. Maybe this is for real. Maybe this is how it starts. I mean, when you're singing in the shower, pretending to be a rock star, you're not actually thinking about how that happens. Scooter definitely had me interested, but what he was talking about sounded like the plot of a movie, not something that happens to a real guy in real life. But Scooter's own life kind of sounded like a movie.

" I'm a 25-year-old guy who used to be one of the most successful party promoters in the country. I decided one day I was never going to throw another party. I just didn't want to be 40 years old saying 'Daddy needs to go to the nightclub.' That's not the life for me. I wanted to be in the music business, be a part of creating something. I went on to become a marketing VP at a record label called So So Def. And then left that job to start my own record label and manage artists. I find new talent and help them build a career. "

'So whose career are you building now?' Mom asked, ready to Google it and call him out if he tried to BS her.

'I just signed a rapper named Asher Roth. He's just getting started, but we've got big plans and I'm excited about his opportunities. I guess, Pattie, the biggest thing you've got to know about me is that I want to make sure your son never has any "what ifs?"'

Scooter ended up winning some points with her over the course of a long conversation. He gave her a long list of impressive references and they just ended up talking about family and morals for about two hours. He seemed like a good guy. Mom said she'd think about it, but she warned me not to get my hopes up.

By this time the YouTube views were up into tens of thousands. One video had been viewed over 72,000 times and had multiple 'honors', which show up when the video is generating a lot of interest. School started in the fall, and, during morning announcements one day, they played a montage of my YouTube videos, which had come to their attention because of Scooter's original phone call. I was still keeping that as sort of a secret identity as far as school was concerned. Kids at school had no idea I did music. They didn't hang out at the tourist places where I was busking. I was almost thirteen and still waiting for a growth spurt. If people knew me at all, they knew me as an athlete. Some of them thought it was their job to put me in my place, and I had a sinking feeling this video montage

"We were talking as if we'd known each other for years"

thing was going to make them even tougher on me.

When Mom finally let me talk to Scooter on the phone, I was like, 'Dude, why did you do that? That was totally embarrassing. Don't you know eighth-graders eat their wounded? I don't need that kind of exposure.'

Scooter laughed, which made me laugh too. After an hour or so, we were talking as if we'd known each other for years. We really are a lot alike in many ways, one of the most important being that we like a lot of the same music.

'Justin,' he said, 'I'm really excited to talk to you. I've spoken to your mom and it looks like she's going to allow me to fly you down to Atlanta on your first flight ever. When you get down here we'll see if you can beat me in HORSE like you claim.' We've been playing HORSE ever since.

'No can do,' I told him. 'We're going to Disney World. I've been saving for the tickets. It's our first vacation, and I'm paying for it.'

He kept working on us, and Mom and I talked it over til late at night.

'This might be an incredible opportunity, Mom. I don't want to screw it up.'

'If this is what you want to do . . .' she nodded, 'let's go to Atlanta. Disney World will still be there when we get back.'

REACH FOR THE SKY

Mom and I boarded our first ever airplane flight in the fall of 2007. We left the ground, went up into the sky. It was every bit as awesome as I'd always thought it would be. All my life I'd been seeing airplanes up in the air, but, when I was a little kid, I thought that was for rich people. I knew it wasn't totally impossible, but people like me and my mom were hardwired to keep our feet on the ground. I guess I saw the music business in kind of the same way. I saw people like Beyoncé, Usher and Justin Timberlake way up there in the stars. Was it even possible that I could do what they do? Scooter seemed to think so, and I wanted to believe it but we kept our feet on the ground. I knew better than to go running my mouth around school until I knew I had something real to talk about. Plus the disappointment of it not becoming real would have been too harsh for me.

When we landed in Atlanta, Scooter showed up to get us at the airport, driving a purple Mercedes. With rims.

I saw it and said, 'Sweet!'

Mom just shook her head. Scooter got out of the car and surprised us with a big hug before he threw our bags in the trunk.

'What's up, guys? I'm Scooter.'

'Glad to meet you. I'm Justin.'

'Nice wheels,' said Mom.

"Scooter was clowning around... we just hit it off straight away"

'This is the first car I ever bought myself,' he told us. 'Paid cash for it back in my party days. I'm a different person now. In a very different line of work. But I still enjoy the car.'

'It's crazy,' I said. 'How's the stereo system?'

'Deafening,' said Scooter.

'Crank it!'

He cranked up the stereo, and I started singing along with Rihanna and Jay-Z on 'Umbrella'. Then Mom started singing along, and pretty soon we were all singing and laughing. Scooter was clowning around, doing his Mike Tyson voice and his Arnold Schwarzenegger voice. We just hit it off right away. Mom couldn't believe it. She was like, 'No one is ever goofy like this with us.'

'If it's okay with you guys, I'm going to head over to Jermaine Dupri's studio,' Scooter said.

'That's definitely okay,' I replied. 'That is sick.'

I knew Jermaine Dupri was big time. Back in the day, he'd launched some extremely successful young performers – rappers Kris Kross, Da Brat and Lil Bow Wow – and since then he'd worked with Mariah Carey, Luther Vandross and Mom's old crushes, Boyz II Men.

'This is just a friendly visit, okay?' Scooter said. 'We're just there to hang out and play some video games. I don't want you to sing for them yet. The plan is to let them get to know you, then show them the videos, then we'll work together on something for you to sing for them. You're not there to audition, understand?'

'I got it.'

We pulled into the parking lot of the private studio, just ahead of a black Range Rover. The driver got out, and my jaw practically dropped to the floor.

'Oh my God! Is that Usher?'

It was the same feeling I had when the airplane took off. I was up in the sky now. I was up there among the stars! It was just nuts, I couldn't believe it. I couldn't wait to see the faces on Chaz and Ryan when I told them I was chillin' out with Usher. Before Scooter could stop me, I was out of the car and across the parking lot.

'Hey, Usher! Hey, man! Oh, man, I love you. Can I sing for you?'

'Nah, little buddy, it's cold out here,' said Usher. 'Let's just go inside.'

People seem to think I met Usher totally by chance in a parking lot in Atlanta, and twenty minutes later I had a record deal. In fact, it was almost a year before I saw Usher again. He totally blew me off, said hello to Scooter and walked into the building to see whoever he was there to see. To this day I still tease Usher about it. He told somebody later he thought I was Scooter's little cousin or something. Ha ha.

As Usher went inside, Scooter looked at me like…Dude!

But he said not to sing for Jermaine Dupri. He never said

"I couldn't wait to see the faces on Chaz and Ryan when I told them I was chillin' out with Usher"

anything about Usher. We went in and met up with JD and played some video games. Every once in a while, I had this great vision of myself telling Chaz and Ryan, 'So there I was chillin' with m'boyz at the studio . . .' Mom was still on high alert, not ready to believe any of this was actually going to go anywhere. We were just goofing around, and I went off on Nelly's rap from 'Grillz', a big song he did with Dupri.

At first, they laughed. It was probably weird to see this little white kid doing Nelly, but then Jermaine said, 'Hold on, hold on. I gotta go get my camera.'

He came back and made me do the whole thing again so he could video it.

'That was extraordinary,' he said when I finished. 'That was crazy. What is this kid — a baby Scooter?'

He laughed in pure amusement — I could tell he and Scooter had a close relationship and that he was enjoying this encounter, but not as much as I was. I mean c'mon, I'm just a kid from Stratford, Ontario, and here I am meeting Jermaine Dupri!

'What he really does is sing,' said Scooter.

Jermaine said, 'This I gotta hear.'

'No, man, not today,' said Scooter. 'He just flew in, and I really haven't had a chance to—'

I let loose a little bit of Boyz II Men. Once again, Scooter just looked at me. Dude!

Jermaine gave Scooter a look.

'It's not going to happen yet, buddy,' Scooter said, laughing and smiling.

I could tell from Scooter's face that it was time to go, that this wasn't part of his plan. Over the years Scooter and me have learned to work in synergy, but we were just starting out together at this point. We went back to the car.

'We're not taking any shortcuts,' Scooter said. 'We're going to plan this carefully and do it right.'

'I don't know about all this,' said Mom. 'I just . . . I wish I knew more about this business. I wish I knew more about you as a person. I mean, you're asking to become a major part of my son's life, a consistent role model. I can't allow that without some kind of . . . I don't know.'

> **"I was up in the sky. I was up there among the stars! It was just nuts"**

'Would it help if you met my family?' asked Scooter.

'Yeah. Actually it would. I'd feel a lot more comfortable.'

'My dad is actually passing through Atlanta tomorrow on his way home from this kite-boarding thing. You'll like him a lot. My dad made me a man. He's my best friend, but I respect him. You'll see. If I'm half the man my dad is, I'm okay.'

The next day, we went to an airport restaurant and met

"Sure he was young, but he was polite and super-motivated. He knew a lot about the business. And he believed in me"

Scooter's dad: Dr. Ervin Braun, a dentist with a flair for extreme sports. Scooter's mom is an orthodontist with a flair for the creative arts. Mom decided this Scooter guy in the purple pimpmobile was okay after all. He had a strong Jewish faith. His family were loving, rock solid and successful. Sure he was young, but he was polite and super-motivated. He knew a lot about the business. And he believed in me.

We were in Atlanta for only a few days, but before we left we formed a plan: we'd continue putting videos up on YouTube, racking up stats and refining what I was doing. Scooter had a lot of ideas about songs I could be singing as well as a strategy on how to present them and involve the growing fan base. They were all songs I loved, so I was completely on board with that. Over the next few months, we'd record new videos and load them up, and Mom and Scooter would stay up all night, watching the numbers climb, counting the honors.

HAPPY NEW YEAR

We spent Christmas 2007 at Grandpa and Grandma's like always. New Year's Eve, we sat there wondering what 2008 would bring.

'I think you should do "With You"', Scooter told me. 'That thing is on fire right now, and I know you can murder it.'

I thought that was a great idea. I loved that song, so it didn't take me long to learn it, and I couldn't wait for Mom to video it. Unfortunately, I'd just gotten the ugliest haircut of my life the day before. My trademark swoosh was hacked off into this squarish situation that kind of reminded me of Bart Simpson. Which was appropriate, because Mom shot the video in my room at Grandpa and Grandma's with the poster of Bart Simpson on the wall behind me. Except the shot is framed so you're just looking at Bart Simpson's crotch. And some little hockey guys. A few minutes into it, I get up and you can see a Tupac poster too, and I guess that sums up my personality – Bart Simpson and Tupac. Ha ha. I don't mind saying, Scooter was right – I really did murder that thing. That was all I cared about. I thought I'd nailed the song and couldn't wait for him to see it.

He was at the Grammys when Mom sent it to him, and he loved the song. But the look – well, not so much. He sent Mom a text message: 'This is really good, but let's shoot again

"In less than a month, that great song with the bad hair hit a million"

when his hair grows back.'

But the text got cut off. All Mom got was 'This is really good', so she loaded it up onto YouTube. By the time Scooter called to tell her to take it down, it had gotten more than 25,000 hits.

'Wow!' he said. 'Well, let's see what happens.'

In less than a month, that great song with the bad hair hit a million.

Now they all hit a million almost immediately, and I can't tell you how grateful I am, but that first one – that was incredibly thrilling.

Mom and Scooter were putting in long nights and hardworking days. Scooter and Carin were going out by then, so poor Carin was sucked into the vortex too. Scooter was flying us down now and then to meet with one person or another, but nobody had the slightest interest in me. We were all getting frustrated. We'd put so much work into this and the YouTube hits were going through the roof, but no one in the 'real-world' music industry cared about that. We kept hearing over and over, 'You can't launch a kid without a TV show. If he's not on Nickelodeon or Disney, forget it.'

Scooter kept trying to tell people, 'This kid already has

a huge fanbase. They're out there. If we give them the records, they'll do the rest.' But that had never been done in the music business. Everyone understood the concept of a viral video, but no one had ever used that to successfully launch a major act. With every person that said 'no', it just seemed to excite Scooter. He said that it would just make it sweeter when it happened.

'Nothing great ever came that easy,' he told me.

Talking to Scooter on the phone late at night, I told him, 'We gotta make this happen. The more I think about it, the more I want it. And, if I say anything about it at school, people think I'm being a jerk.'

'They're just jealous,' said Scooter.

'Of what? They think I'm making the whole thing up. They're like, "If you're all that, when are you gonna be on MTV, Bieber?"; "Hey, Bieb, aren't you supposed to be at Neverland having lunch with Michael Jackson?"'

'Maybe they're jealous because you have something to believe in.'

I hadn't thought of that.

'This is going to happen, Justin,' he told me. 'The only thing that can stop you is you. People who fail in this business – the really talented people, I mean – it's never about the music. It's about their personal lives. Stay focused and never mind any of the crap anybody says. That's not you, that's them. That's the negative place they want to live in. You choose to live in a positive place.'

"Nothing great ever came that easy"

CHAPTER 5

THE START OF A NEW LIFE

justinbieber dont believe dreams come true? Think about this - Im following more people on Twitter than live in my entire hometown. Dreams do come true

5:08 AM Apr 30th via web

The pre-show VIP meet'n'greet is an opportunity for me to hang out with a few fans before the rest of the crowd move in. Opening night of the tour, about two hundred beautiful girls gather right in front of the stage. My DJ, Tay James, joins me onstage and gets things going. He really knows how to light the fire. Dan comes out and we jam on a little 'Crazy Train', and then I call for Scooter.

'Give it up for my manager, Scooter Braun!'

Fans love it when I drag Scooter out. As a manager, he can solve any problem that comes up – untie any knot, fix any mistake – but he's also one of the most creative people I've ever met. He does impersonations that are dead-on hilarious. The girls down front go crazy. They all know who he is.

'Scooter, come on out here. Do Schwarzenegger. Please? C'mon. Do it.'

He takes a mike and says, 'Buy da ahlbum of Jostin Beebah or I break your arm off and beat you with it.'

Everybody falls out laughing, and he switches to

Mike Tyson.

'I jutht want to thay . . . Juthtin Bieber hath made me one leth lonely guy.'

'Obama! Scooter, do Obama.' He tries to wave it off and walk away, but I get the crowd chanting, 'Obama! Obama! Obama!'

'Well, as you know, it's all about change. My lovely daughters, Sasha and Malia, are big fans of this guy right here. And I gotta tell ya, I love the Bieb.'

We do some Q&A. It's mostly the usual questions, but I don't mind, because everyone is in such a great mood. The energy is already building.

Scooter waves his hand at the back of the group.

'Yes, you. Old guy back there. You had a question?'

'Yeah,' he says. 'Do you have any special guests coming tonight?'

'Well, let's see,' I reply. 'I've got my mom here, of course, and my grandpa and grandma. And then there's my good friend—'

Before I can say Usher's name, the crowd catch sight of him coming out on stage behind me. The place goes bananas. Usher gives me a sideways bro hug. We do one of our famous

"Scooter's one of the most creative people I've ever met"

"This is the first step to forever"

secret handshakes. He waves before he goes backstage to crazy applause.

Dan and I wrap things up. The VIP fans head to a reception upstairs. The arena is quiet for the moment. Under the stage Usher and I sit on the edge of a ramp, talking quietly.

'The successful journey starts with the first step,' he tells me. 'And obviously that first step is the hardest. It's a lot to ask of someone so young to take on such an incredible feat. You've got to pace yourself. Enjoy yourself. Go out there and know that all this hard work has paid off, and this is the moment for you to enjoy it.'

'I will,' I reply. 'Everybody's been busting on me all week about voice rest, but we need to rehearse. I want everything to go right. I don't want to let anybody down.'

'You know the energy of this entire family. Everything's very loose, very organic, a lot of love. We're trying to care for you. Obviously your voice is the most important part. They can't listen to the music when they're watching you dance, so we've got to protect that voice, and that's really why I wanted to be here for the first run. I want to make sure you understand that you've got to pace yourself. It's not gonna all happen over one show. Think about the eighty-five shows coming up.'

'That's all I've been thinking about, man. Are you kidding? Eighty-five shows in six months. I get it.'

"I want everything to go right. I don't want to let anyone down"

'Eighty-five seems very big. Intimidating. But the first step is the reality of it coming to an end someday. And when you get to number eighty-five you'll be so seasoned, you'll be recognized then as being a forever artist – not a flash in the pan – and the next step is a major world tour. This is the first step to forever, man. It'll go as far as you want to. But you have to be smart. You'll have to pace yourself onstage and in life.'

That was a tough lesson for me to learn when I was trying to break into this business. Patience. Pacing. But we made it happen. After that 'With You' video with the bad hair and Bart Simpson's crotch, the next video we posted to my YouTube channel was me singing for Usher in February of 2008.

A FRIEND FOR LIFE

The way this all happened kind of reminded me of *Horton Hears a Who!* Scooter is the elephant, trying to tell all the kangaroos and cockatoos in the music business that there are a zillion fans out there, but nobody would believe him for the longest time. He decided we needed some star power on our side. We needed to go into these record-label meetings with somebody who had some flash and could give that stamp. Scooter knew two guys who were perfect for this job: Justin Timberlake and Usher. They'd both made it big as teens, and then went on to make the successful transition to major stars as adults. They're both nice

guys, who get big respect from label executives. We managed to get both of them to look at the videos on YouTube, which by now really demonstrated how much I was growing – physically and vocally – and how many fans were just waiting for me to put something out there.

Usher said to Scooter, 'Where has this kid been? Why haven't I seen him?'

'You did,' said Scooter. 'That was him in the parking lot that day. Remember? He wanted to sing for you.'

'Man, everybody wants to sing. How was I supposed to know he's the real thing?'

Timberlake had the same reaction. Both he and Usher

were interested in meeting me right away. There was no way Mom and I could keep our feet on the ground now. It was like, Usher and Timberlake want to meet me? Are you kidding? There was no point in trying to tell anyone at school about this. It would be like telling them I was going to meet CHUCK NORRIS, and we all know that guy is untouchable. I mean, c'mon. It's CHUCK NORRIS. He doesn't need Twitter, he's already following you.

Two weeks before my fourteenth birthday, Mom and I flew to Atlanta to meet Usher. I stood there in my Toronto Maple Leafs hoody and sang 'You Got It Bad' for him. He sat there in his leather jacket and listened. We sat around and talked for a while, and he was one of the coolest people I'd ever met. He gives off this great, calm, friendly vibe that just makes you feel glad to be there. Mom liked him a lot, and we were both over the moon when Scooter told us he wanted me to come back so we could talk about possible ways to work together, but Scooter told him, 'We still have to have this conversation with Timberlake. I promised I'd bring the kid to meet him.'

We met up with Justin Timberlake at his place in Memphis. Jessica Biel was there. Scooter practically had to put his hands over my eyes to make me stop looking at her. Timberlake arrived, and I sang 'Cry Me a River' for him.

'It takes a lot of balls to sing me my own song,' he said. But I guess he liked me, because he wanted to move forward with

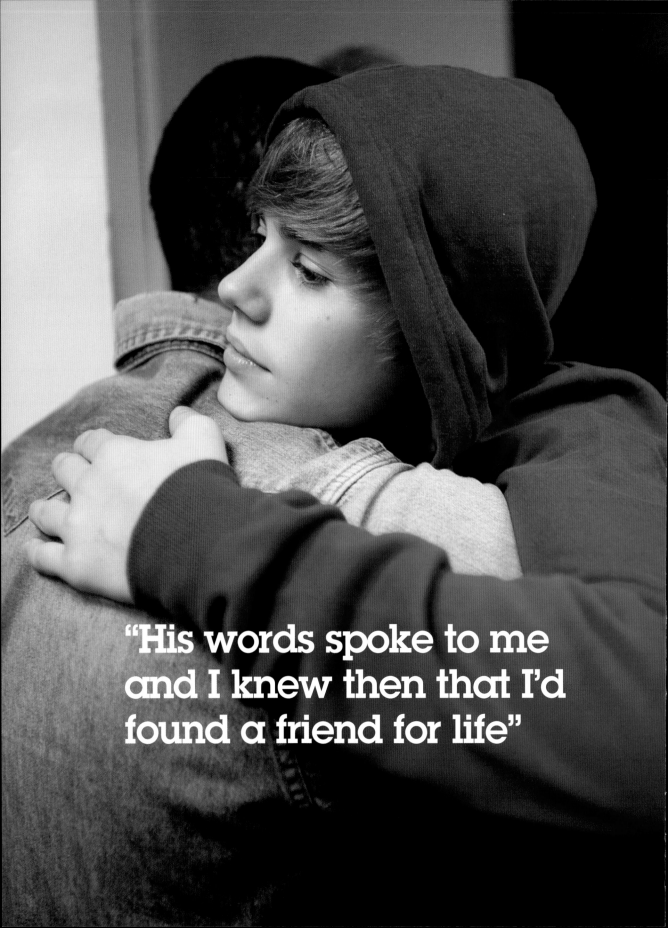

"His words spoke to me and I knew then that I'd found a friend for life"

a deal and we spent the rest of the afternoon just hanging out watching March Madness basketball together. Timberlake was and still is just an amazing talent, and someone to this day I look up to and study his career. It was so surreal that he wanted to do a deal with me, just a kid from a small town in Canada. And so did Usher.

I couldn't believe things were finally coming together. I was almost afraid to believe it. The only thing I can compare it to is when I bungee-jumped off a bridge in New Zealand not long ago. It was a long journey to get there, but, at the last minute, there I was. Standing there. Ready. I had no idea what this was going to be like, but I knew it was going to be awesome.

Mom and I flew down to Atlanta again, and Usher put us up in a super-fancy hotel that was like a different universe from anywhere I'd ever been. There were phones by the toilet and a safe in a drawer. The refrigerator was stocked with everything kids love to eat, and there was a huge basket of toys in my room. I got out a Rubik's Cube and worked it out in about three minutes. (There's a trick to it.) When I handed it to Usher, he looked at Scooter and said, 'Who is this kid?'

When Usher talks to you one on one, he speaks very quietly, but he's very intense and his eyes never break away from yours. When he talked to me and Mom, he spoke with a lot of passion and

"They're like tag-team wrestlers"

made a lot of sense.

'If you're an astronaut going to the moon, there's not a whole lot of people in the world with whom you can share that experience. Well, I'm a fellow astronaut. I've been to the moon. I can talk you up and get you back down safely. The beautiful part of all this is you don't get a chance to see it while you're in it. Now I actually get a chance to step back and watch it all happen again. Those incredible moments on stage . . . Even the obstacles, it'll be a pleasure to watch, even though it's agonizing, you know. But I can be more helpful because I've experienced that. Being the entertainer I am, I stand on the shoulders of giants that basically were trailblazers. And all of my experiences, I want to share. All my knowledge. I want to share it with you and help you make this moment happen.'

His words spoke to me, and I knew then that I'd found a friend for life. We made the decision to go forward with Usher, and I've never doubted it for a second. I'm the luckiest guy on earth to have him as my wingman.

Scooter and Usher formed a partnership to navigate my career, and that seemed like a perfect idea. There's a lot Scooter can tell me, and I trust him, but he doesn't know what it's like for me dealing with living in the spotlight the way Usher does. They're like tag-team wrestlers, only instead of bashing me over the head with folding chairs they make me drink lots of water.

THE REAL DEAL

When Usher talks, people listen. He called the guy who'd given him his start, L.A. Reid, CEO of Island Def Jam Music Group. This is the music-industry legend who launched Mariah Carey, Pink, Avril Lavigne, TLC, Outkast, Toni Braxton and a whole lot of other Grammy winners and multi-platinum mega-artists. The dude is a beast. In April 2008, Mom and I met Scooter and Usher in New York City for what I knew might be one of the most important moments of my life. Getting signed to a record deal at Island Def Jam – that was the Holy Grail. We'd really be on our way. I couldn't let myself think about it too much or I'd have been totally psyched out.

I'd seen the movie *August Rush* a few days earlier and loved that part where the kid is playing that crazy slap-style guitar with the guitar lying down flat, and he's wailing on it like it's a guitar and drums and piano all at once. (Check it out on YouTube. It's sick.) I channeled all my nervous energy into figuring out how to do it. The morning of the meeting, I couldn't keep still. I was slamming away on that slap-style guitar, and Scooter shot a video of me so we could throw it up on YouTube and share it with my fans.

In the car on the way to the meeting, I was still slapping and drumming on my lap, humming, making bad jokes, driving Mom crazy. Finally we were walking into L.A. Reid's office with

justinbieber It's wild..this was the morning I got signed just 2 years ago. very grateful

2.53 PM Apr13th via web

Chris Hicks from Def Jam, a man who was to have a big part to play in shaping my career and who has supported me every step of the way. L.A.'s office was like a cathedral – if a cathedral had cigars on the table. The walls were covered with pictures of music history: him laughing with Stevie Wonder and Lionel Ritchie, him at the Grammys with one gigantic hit maker after another, him shaking hands with President Obama. Huge windows look out over New York City. The sofas were white as piano keys. I was afraid to sit down.

L.A. Reid is totally the most suave individual in the world. His designer suit was sharp enough to put your eye out. He said, 'C'mon in. Nice to meet you, young man.'

He sat behind his desk, which was bigger than Grandpa's car. Scooter and Usher pushed seats out of the way, and I stood in the middle of the room with my guitar and sang a of couple songs. Scooter said, 'Do the *August Rush* thing.'

I did that too, and then I stood there waiting.

Finally, L.A. said, 'Wow!'

He picked up the phone and made a few calls. In about thirty seconds, six more people came in and sat on the white sofas.

'Do it again,' he said, and you better believe I did.

We thanked everybody. Everybody thanked us. They left. Then we left. I guess, if life was a movie, the director would say, drama? Where's the big moment?' But it just doesn't work like that. The way it works is you go to these meetings, and then you go home and wait and wait and wait…and still wait for the phone to ring until you hear that you're going to take the next small step forward. Or not.

Mom and I went back to Stratford, jumped out of our skin every time the phone rang, and finally − finally − got the amazing news we'd been waiting for. Island Def Jam wanted to sign me. I was on top of the world, but Scooter said, 'Keep your shirt on. This is huge, but we've got to work through the details before we celebrate.'

"Island Def Jam wanted to sign me. I was on top of the world."

It would take another whole book to try to explain the business side of all this, but Scooter wanted me to understand it, so he made me sit in. Didn't matter if I was falling asleep, tapping my feet, going insane from boredom, he wanted me to know what was going on. There was only one thing I really wanted to know: 'Do I get a tour bus?'

'Eventually,' said Scooter. 'I definitely see that down the road.'

'Yes! Will the bus have an Xbox?'

Scooter laughed and said, 'That's the dream.'

Long story short, the paperwork was finally worked out, and Mom and I flew to Atlanta. The night we officially signed the deal with Def Jam, Scooter took us all out to Straits, this restaurant owned by Ludacris. Scooter's other artist Asher Roth and his buddy Boyder came along, and kept teasing me about toasting with ginger ale while everyone else had champagne and how they could still beat me playing *Rock Band* and *Guitar Hero*, even if I was in the big leagues now. Asher was really blowing up huge on the rap scene right then, the rising star everybody (including Eminem) was talking about.

He was like, 'I'm gonna watch you, bro. I don't want you splashing money around and getting into the nice things. You gotta stay humble about it.'

'It's cool, Asher. I'll just have people walking behind throwing flower petals everywhere I go,' I joked.

Scooter had the kitchen send out a big chocolate cake, and, when it came to the table, he stood up and announced to the whole place, 'Everybody? Hey, may I have your attention, please? This young man has just signed a record deal with Island Def Jam!'

This was Atlanta, musical center of the universe, in a restaurant owned by Ludacris. Everybody sitting there knew how huge this was. The whole place broke out in cheers and whistling.

It was embarrassing — like when the waiters come out and sing 'Happy Birthday' or whatever — but, after all we'd been through together, it was a great moment. We'd really gotten to be a family.

"There was only one thing
I really wanted to know:
'Will the bus have an Xbox?'"

That made it a little easier to think about leaving Stratford. Mom and I went home and started making plans to move to Atlanta. Neither of us could believe how far we'd come. And it blew both our minds to think about how far we might go.

I was eager to get on with it. I was writing songs and playing music all the time, dying to get into the recording studio, itching with that about-to-bungee-jump-off-a-bridge feeling. I tried to keep my mouth shut about it at school, because here's the thing about telling people you're about to bungee-jump off a bridge — or do anything else that seems different or big or outside of what people usually do — your real friends will be like, 'Dude! That's awesome!' Other people will look at you like you're an idiot and point out all the things that might go wrong. And the people who are the least happy with their own lives will hope that the cord breaks and you fracture your skull.

But, as Scooter said, that's about them, not you.

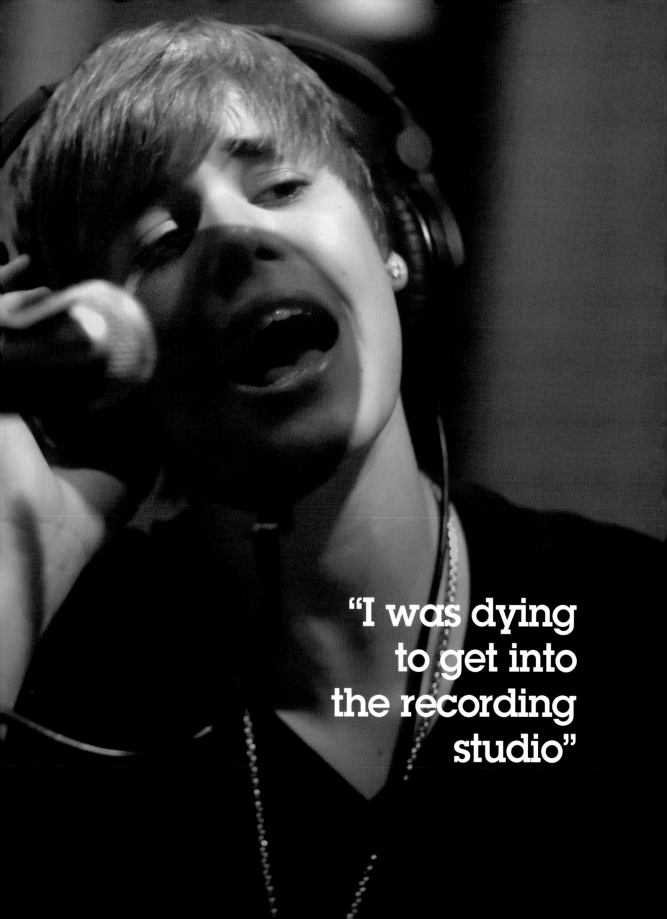

"I was dying
to get into
the recording
studio"

A MOVING EXPERIENCE

I spent another summer busking in front of the Avon Theatre and started ninth grade at Northwestern Secondary School, still waiting for that growth spurt, competing with the twelfth-grade athletes, the Goliaths.

Mom worked through all the paperwork you need to move to the United States from Canada, which is a lot more complicated than you might think. She sold all our stuff, and we moved in with Grandpa and Grandma, which was probably more fun for me than it was for Mom and Grandma. Nerves got frayed.

Weeks turned into months. This was probably the hardest part of the whole thing: waiting. And waiting. And waiting. Finally, everything was in place. We said goodbye to Grandpa and Grandma and all our friends – everything we'd ever thought of as home – and headed for Atlanta with nothing but our clothes and my guitar.

Carin and Scooter went scouting around Asher's neighborhood and found a house for us a block from his place so we'd be able to hang out. It was all so last minute Scooter even had to sign the lease for the house in his name so we didn't end up

"Mama Jan has become one of the most important people in my life"

losing the place. Our first night in town, we stayed with Carin's mom and dad, and the next day Scooter took us shopping and let Mom put furniture and other household necessities on his credit card.

Now it was time to get down to business.

Usher set me up with Jan Smith – Mama Jan – who also happens to be his vocal coach. She only takes on big acts, but she took me on because Usher pleaded my case. She's one of the greatest people in the whole world, like a second mom to all of us, and she's become one of the most important people in my life. She doesn't mess around, and I don't even think about pranking her or pulling any kind of crap.

Another question people ask me all the time is if my career will fall apart if my voice changes.

'There's no if about it,' Jan said right from the start. 'Puberty happens. We'll work through it.'

I'm not worried. She got Usher through it, too. And she brought him back after he'd completely lost his voice.

Scooter says she's our secret sauce.

The next important member to join the family was Jenny, my tutor. Because I was only fourteen, there were strict child-labor laws that governed the hours I was allowed to work and educational requirements that had to be followed to the letter. Jenny works for the School of Young Performers, which specializes in homeschooling kids and teenagers who work in the entertainment industry. This was the school that Chris Brown and Rihanna and lots of kids in Broadway theater and television used.

Jenny and I do pretty good together. (Pretty well, that is. Holla, Jenny!) She makes sure I'm on top of the homework and stuff, and I don't prank her more than once a month. It's hard to resist, because she's so sweet and believes everything I say, which makes her very prankable.

On April Fools' Day, I said to her, 'Hey, Jenny, let's do a science experiment.'

'Great idea,' she said. 'Let's do it.'

'I read that if you put salt on top of butter, it heats it up. You can actually feel it.'

'Really? I've never heard that.'

I carefully put a stick of butter on a plate and measured a tablespoon of salt over it.

'Okay, now we have to wait sixty seconds.' I meticulously timed the sixty seconds, then held my hand over the butter. 'Oh, that's wild. You really can feel it. That's amazing. Check it out.'

Jenny held her palm over the plate of butter, and faster than she could react, I pushed her hand down and squished the butter all over.

It was hysterical.

Pranks vs school = pranks win all day. Can you blame me? I'm just a kid.

justinbieber SCHOOL!!! she thinks im typing my paper right now. Lol

11:51 AM Feb 12th via web

justinbieber Got caught...education is the key

12.13 PM Feb 12th via web

FIGURING IT OUT

There was a lot of back-and-forth over whether or not I was ready to go into the studio and record my first single. Usher felt my voice was raw and needed more Mama Jan, but Scooter and I were impatient. We were beginning to think I'd go through puberty and grow a beard before I ever got anything on tape.

Scooter had a woman named Tashia working with him as an A&R administrator on certain projects, helping him organize producers and cutting the payments and everything, but Tashia also has her own studio with Lashaunda 'Babygirl' Carr. Asher Roth had worked there a few times and liked it a lot.

Scooter told me and Mom, 'I think this would be a great place for Justin creatively. It's not scary. There are no bad influences.'

Mom liked the sound of all that, and I liked the sound of their music. One song in particular seemed perfect for me. They played 'Common Denominator' for us, and Scooter said, 'This is the song.'

Out of all the things in life that I could fear,
The only thing that would hurt me is if you
weren't here,
I don't want to go back to just being one half
of the equation

It had all the heart and soul we were looking for, plus the math images that make you think of a guy and a girl sitting close together helping each other with homework.

So before we had any real budget or plan or album in the works, I got in there and recorded it, and I found out I loved being in the studio. Not as much as performing live, but a lot. The night we finished it, Carin was going to drive me home, but we ended up driving around and around Atlanta, listening to my song over and over. We stopped for ice cream at some point, but I think we drove around until about three in the morning. To this day it's still Carin's favorite song, and she constantly tells me I have to sing it someday at her wedding. It was a great song. What killed me was not being able to put it out into the world. We had to be very strategic about the first single to be released.

Mama Jan had a showcase for all her acts a couple times a year at Eddie's Attic, the place where John Mayer was discovered. Mama Jan invited me to sing. So at the end of the program, after all these amazing acts who'd been training with her for years, I got up and sang 'Common Denominator'. At the end of it, everyone was on their feet, and I was pretty much in shock. (The video's on YouTube. Check out that look on my face.)

Scooter sent 'Common Denominator' up to L.A. Reid, sent it over to Usher, sent it to everybody, saying, 'It's time to record.'

And they were like, 'Yeah. It's time.'

Usually, people record ten songs or so, release them on an album, and follow with another album a year later. Scooter and L.A.'s idea was to do a dozen songs plus bonus tracks and divide them between two albums – *My World* and *My World 2.0* – releasing them only about four months apart. We dove into the studio. I've never worked so hard in my life – and I've never had so much fun.

One night, Scooter was driving me home, and I was lovin' on this music he was playing. It was just the skeleton of a song – like a demo the songwriter records just to give you a general idea.

'This is awesome,' I told Scooter. 'Who is this guy?'

He said, 'It's Adonis. He's a writer. An artist too, but he writes for people.'

'Cool, cool. Who'd he write this one for?' I asked.

'You.'

"I'd never worked so hard in my life – and I'd never had so much fun"

I was totally in shock. Speechless. Because I felt like, if I tried to talk, I was going to start bawling. You have to understand, I was still so new to this and the thought of all these amazing people writing these songs with me in mind was overwhelming. Even now I still feel that way whenever someone I look up to in the music industry wants to work with me. I'm just so grateful. I hope to never lose that feeling. Scooter cranked it up louder, and when we got to my house, he kept on driving so we could keep listening to it again and again.

'Overboard . . .'

I just couldn't believe this great song was mine. We laid it down, and I loved it. Later on, we recut it with Jessica Jarrell, and I loved it even more. Finally, we had ten songs recorded. Among them were 'One Time', 'Down to Earth' and 'One Less Lonely Girl'. I could never tell you which ones were my favorites: I was proud of each and every track.

Now it was time to go back to L.A. Reid and persuade him to get behind us and release *My World* in a big way.

CHAPTER 6

WELCOME TO MY WORLD

In January 2009, Scooter went to Los Angeles for the Grammys. His first stop was L.A. Reid's bungalow at the Beverly Hills Wilshire.

'What's a bungalow?' I had to ask.

'Someday, young Padawan. Someday, you will know the bungalow.'

'Whatever. Tell me what happened.'

'Well, for starters, one of his key people is walking me over to the bungalow – which is like your own little house within this luxury hotel where he always stays – and she says, "I just wanted to tell you how proud I am, couldn't happen to a better group of guys," and so on. "I'm so happy for you," she says. "But you have to understand, L.A. is a music guy. He has his own speakers flown out to freakin' Los Angeles to this bungalow every year. And, if you get to play three records for him, that's amazing. If he only listens to one, don't be mad." I said okay. She said, "How many you gonna play?" I said ten. She said, "You're not gonna play ten. Pick the best three and play those." I said okay.'

'Wait, wait, wait!' I said. Sometimes Scooter gets going on a story and leaves me behind. 'Which three did you play?'

'The best three.'

'Yeah, but—'

'No, listen. He goes, "This is great stuff. I wasn't expecting it to be, like, that's a hit, that's a hit, that's a hit."'

'Which three?'

'It doesn't matter. Because he listened to all ten. And then he listened to them all again,' he said.

'He listened to ten songs twice?'

'He listened to ten songs…twice.'

'That's – wow! So what happens now?'

'You get your butt out here and sell this with me tomorrow.'

Shortly after, I was back on the white sofa, listening to my music with L.A. Reid. Crazy. He asked Scooter what we wanted to do, and Scooter asked for a small budget to make a video. Asher Roth had blown up huge on the Internet over the last year with the #1 album on iTunes for ten straight days and #5 album on Billboard Hot 100. Asher was the biggest thing on the Internet. L.A. asked Scooter if he thought I could make it as big as that. Without missing a beat, Scooter said, 'He already is bigger, you just don't know it yet. This kid's like a sleeping giant.'

We called Usher in to help us out on the video for 'One Time'. The storyline is basically me hijacking Usher's house for a party. We flew my best friend Ryan 'Butsy' Butler to Atlanta so he could be in on the shoot. (That's him playing video games with me at the beginning.) When the rest of the cast showed up the whole party was full of beautiful, nice, fun – did I say gorgeous? – girls our age. Dancing, tossing confetti, swimming in bikinis.

'Oh . . . dude . . .' Ryan seemed to have trouble breathing at times. 'This is sick.'

'Just act cool, buddy. It's going to be a long day.'

The video turned out great, and we had a blast making it. The plan was to put it out there on a Tuesday morning a few weeks after the single was released. There would be promotional banners running for the first few days on iTunes, announcing this awesome new video by a new artist, featuring Usher. Good plan, huh?

But that's not what happened. Through some kind of mix-up somewhere in the pipeline, 'One Time' accidentally went into the iTunes system two weeks early, late on a Friday night, with no banner ads, no promotional page – nada. You literally had to go on your iTunes and type in Justin Bieber to see the icon for the video. If you didn't search on it specifically, you'd never know it was there. And, since no one knew it was there, no one was going to search on it.

Scooter was so angry it was almost scary. He wrote an irate email to everybody involved in this thing at every level, and they all wrote back saying how sorry they were. He got quiet for a while (which is pretty unusual for Scooter), then he smiled at me and said: 'I'm not really angry. We can make this work to our advantage. The kids are going to find it.'

We'd just set up my Facebook page, so we posted a message on that. We'd set up a Twitter account a couple weeks earlier and sent out my very first tweet:

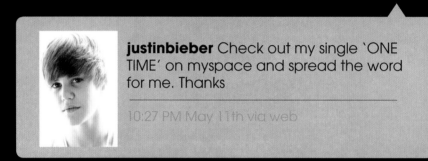

justinbieber Check out my single 'ONE TIME' on myspace and spread the word for me. Thanks

10:27 PM May 11th via web

I got on there and started tweeting my brains out. I followed all my followers and friended their friends. I replied and retweeted and commented and tweeted back and forth as the conversation got bigger and bigger.

Monday morning, 'One Time' was the #3 video on iTunes, stomping up the list over some of the biggest acts in the world. It was mind-blowing; we'd made it. We'd proved we could do it.

Tuesday morning, it was #2 behind Taylor Swift (and I'd never complain about being a runner-up behind Taylor Swift. She has been supporting me since day one and is still an amazing friend).

Wednesday, Thursday, Friday, we hung in there.

"If I can do just one-tenth of the good Michael Jackson did for others, I can really make a difference in this world"

And the following week…the King himself, Michael Jackson, died.

Somebody sent me a text. Feeling like I'd been kicked in the gut, I texted Scooter: 'Dude, Michael Jackson died?'

Scooter messaged back that people were always spreading jacked-up rumors about Michael. No way was he really dead. But he was. It was on the news. It was all over the Internet.

I was devastated. One of my greatest idols, and my inspiration, was gone. Of course, everything he ever recorded went straight to the top of the charts on iTunes, because he's the King, which in turn meant that everyone else was driven off for weeks. 'One Time' the single went to #14, hovering in the top 20 with a few big names and all those Michael Jackson songs that had been part of my life's soundtrack since I was born. It was a weird feeling. 'One Time' the video stayed in the top ten with Taylor and all those amazing videos by Michael, one of the great music-video artists of all time.

We have a special moment in the *My World 2.0* touring show that works as a celebration of Michael Jackson and a good

"My team is my family and they all deserve their time to shine too"

reminder for me about what matters in this business. To the beat of 'Wanna Be Startin' Something', I get to introduce my dance crew and bandmates one by one, so that everybody on the stage gets a good round of applause. My team is my family and they all deserve their time to shine too.

We wanted a strong charity component to this tour, and that's partly a tribute to the example set for us by Michael Jackson. A dollar of every ticket sold goes to Pencils of Promise, an organization that builds desperately needed schools in developing world countries. And it adds up fast. In the second leg of the tour alone, we're building fifteen schools around the world. Michael Jackson was the most giving artist of all time. If I can do just one-tenth of the good he did for others, I can really make a difference in this world. That's what this is all about.

MY WOLF PACK

Over the summer of 2009, we released my first four singles, even though it's kind of unusual to have that many singles before you release an album. We were getting a lot of attention on YouTube and iTunes, but we weren't getting the radio play necessary for a successful album. So many people were still locked into thinking that someone my age couldn't get radio play, that you had to be on Nickelodeon or Disney. We had to change that way of thinking. Scooter and two of my champions at Island Def Jam, Steve Bartels and Erik Olesen, decided there was only one way to fight those old ideas: hand-to-hand combat. Basically, we had to go to every radio station on Planet Earth and make them play my records. We were hoping we could do this with our natural charm and charisma, but we were ready to call in CHUCK NORRIS if needed.

This sounded like a great idea to me, but it was hard to leave Atlanta. We'd only just gotten settled. I had a little papillon pup named Sammy, and I was seeing a girl I really liked. I'd also become good friends with Asher Roth and that crew. He was one step ahead of me in the business and had learned a lot of things the hard way. I absorbed a lot of that just hanging out at their house (which was just a block from mine) playing the music video game *Rock Band*. Asher had blown up pretty big by this time, so he was gone on tour most of the time, too.

'Do what you need to do,' he advised me. 'This is the moment.'

What we needed to do, according to Scooter, was go anywhere we were asked to go and do our music for anyone who wanted to hear it. For free. Any time. Any place.

Usher felt that I needed another influence to guide me in the industry and develop my look, so we brought Ryan Good on board to be my stylist and temporary road manager. For a while, everyone was calling Ryan Good my 'swagger coach' – which he hated almost as much as 'stylist', which isn't at all what he does for me. Style is such a broad word. Style can be how you carry yourself and how you wear whatever you have on. I like to consider my style as very relatable. Usually I'm in blue jeans and a hoody, and the rest is in my attitude. I don't know if it's possible to 'style' another person. I mean, a stylist can tell you what clothes to wear, but the attitude is up to you. I don't know what the word would be, but Ry Good keeps my head on straight so I don't come off like a douchebag. Mostly he's a friend who's honest with me. Everybody should have at least one of those, and I'm fortunate to have several.

"We were ready to call in CHUCK NORRIS if needed"

"Ryan's a friend who's honest with me. Everybody should have at least one of those"

It started out with just me and a guitar. Me, Mom and Ryan, traveling all across North America playing for different radio stations. Then we started doing some shopping malls and amusement parks and stuff like that, so Scooter decided we needed dancers. We flew to LA, where a lot of the best dancers reside, and found two great guys, Antonio and Marvin. At first I didn't know if I wanted them to be part of my wolf pack. But as soon as I got to know them, I definitely wanted them to be part of my wolf pack. We worked up choreography for our first big performance in Kansas City. We were getting more requests to do more shows, so we were able to bring in our DJ, Tay James. He also soon became part of my wolf pack

We were scheduled to appear at a mall in Toronto, and, when we first got to the store, there were two or three people in there. We sent out a message on Twitter, saying where we were, and ten minutes later about forty people showed up. Mall security kept things in line as long as they could, but pretty soon there were a couple of hundred people lined up to get into the store. They ended up blocking one whole wing of the mall so I could get out.

While we were performing in Canada, we decided to add another guitar player and start doing acoustic performances. That's how we got Dan Kanter. I was really unsure about hiring

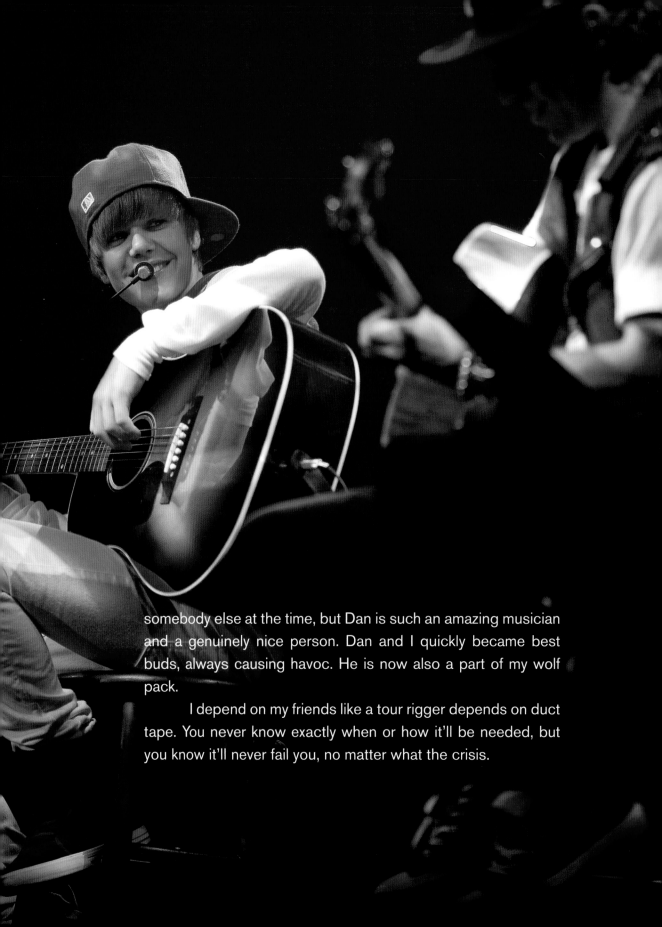

somebody else at the time, but Dan is such an amazing musician and a genuinely nice person. Dan and I quickly became best buds, always causing havoc. He is now also a part of my wolf pack.

I depend on my friends like a tour rigger depends on duct tape. You never know exactly when or how it'll be needed, but you know it'll never fail you, no matter what the crisis.

STRAIGHT TALKING

There's a huge difference between where I was a year ago and where I am now. We could see where we were and where we needed to be. Ry Good is one of the people who helped draw the line between the two.

That was our little group a year ago, playing for forty people in the rain at the Poughkeepsie Water Park. We got up at three in the morning to be on early radio and TV shows. We sat in airports for hours, jamming and writing songs between flights. We did interviews day after day, hearing the same jokes about my hair and my size and my age.

Just for future reference, here are some of the questions that will get an actual conversation going for me:

- **When people ask about my family and if I have brothers or sisters.** (I'm a proud big brother, ready to brag about how great Jaxon and Jazmyn are.)
- **When people ask what my favorite musical instrument is.** (I play trumpet in addition to guitar, piano, and drums, and I'm ready to talk music anytime, anywhere.)
- **When people ask what's on my iPod.** (I'm always listening to something new and interesting because everyone I meet turns me on to an artist I haven't heard of. I like everything from Tupac to Canadian bands like Tragically Hip.)
- **When people ask about where I come from.** (Oh, Canada! I stand on guard for thee!)
- **When people ask me about my travels.** (Nothing cracks your mind wide open like experiencing cultures that differ from your own. I've learned to respect cultures that used to seem strange and eat some freaky new foods.)
- **When people ask me about schooling and how I get it done.** (Gives me an opening to tell about the latest prank I've pulled on Jenny.)
- **When people ask me who inspired me.** (A long list starting with Usher and Grandpa.)
- **When people ask me about my religion.** (Because I love God, and I don't want to miss an opportunity to share that.)

I really like...

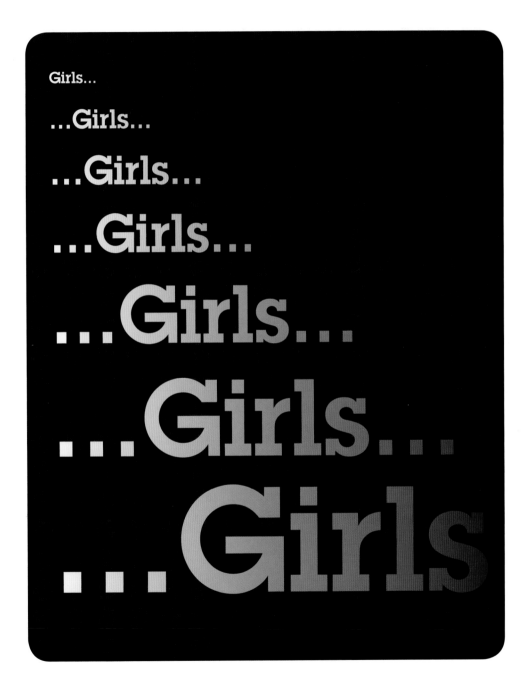

Girls...

...Girls...

...Girls...

...Girls...

...Girls...

...Girls...

...Girls

Nah, I'm joking. I don't mean that. There are lots of things I really like besides girls. Like pizza. And pranking. And CHUCK NORRIS. You probably knew I was joking, but not everybody does. Here's a clue, just for future reference. If you have to ask me if I'm being serious, I'm not. In fact, you seldom get a straight answer from anyone around here. If you ask the tour riggers what they do, TJ will tell you he's a brain surgeon and Phildeaux will say he's with the city's sanitation department. Ask Scooter what his job is, and he'll say Roadie. If you ask me how tall I am, I'll say 'seven feet'. We kid around. And we love it.

"We kid around.
And we love it"

BREAKING GROUND

Last summer, wherever we went, fans followed, and we were always happy to see them. Word would get out on Twitter, and a crowd would gather on the street outside the radio station or the parking lot outside a bowling alley, fairground, mall, you name it.

It was crazy, but by this time Kenny joined the crew as my bodyguard. He was an Atlanta DJ who'd become a good friend. When Scooter was out of town with Asher, I'd get a little bit crazy cooped up in the house with my mom all the time, so Kenny would take me wherever I needed to go or just pick me up to go bowling or to play laser tag. Gearing up for the radio tour, Scooter decided there was no one on this earth we could trust and depend on as we could trust and depend on Kenny, so he sent Kenny off to get trained and certified in personal security.

By the time we'd finished the radio tour it was clear that Scooter's strategy about how to launch me had worked – we had four consecutive hit singles even before *My World* came out as an album. First time for any artist – ever.

Everything about the way *My World* was released turned the old way of thinking inside out. A skinny white kid on a record with rappers with serious street cred. A teen fan favorite with no TV show. Marketing experts at the label told us we could

"Kenny would take me
wherever I needed to go
or just pick me up to go
bowling or to play laser tag"

"It all happened because of you"

expect to move 60,000 in five weeks. We ended up selling 900,000 in five weeks.

I'm sure me and the team would love to take credit for this, but the truth of it is that it all happened because of you. We are good, but we aren't that good, and every day I wake up knowing I have the best fans in the world. Every day you go above and beyond for me, and I know I'm going off the storyline but I wanted to let you know that *I know* and I'm extremely appreciative every day.

Back to the story.

When my songs hit the charts in Canada, my grandpa and grandma were incredibly proud and excited. That's been one of the greatest things about all this. It's exciting in all the ways you'd expect it to be, but it was a great feeling to make my family so proud – and to be able to help them. It's amazing to think about actually being able to buy a nice house for my mom.

We were way too busy to get cocky about it, but we started to realize how huge our fanbase really was. The week *My World* was released, we had an event scheduled at a mall in Long Island. Long story short, the place was a total mob scene. Thousands of fans showed up, and security was overwhelmed before I even got there. The event had to be cancelled for the safety of the fans, which is of course, a top priority for Scooter and me and everyone

justinbieber Sometimes this is the most fun ever. other times its really hard and theres so much pressure. Thanks 2 everyone for the support. means a lot

5:32 PM Apr 14th via web

on our team. Even though we weren't there and did our best to help handle the situation, two people from our team got arrested. It was crazy. Media reports kept comparing it to Beatlemania. Suddenly, the whole world was paying attention.

Offers started coming in from all over. German TV show? Sure! Japanese record store? We're there! Bungee-jumping off a bridge in New Zealand? We are so there!

During the second half of 2009, we traveled all over the world, seeing so many beautiful places, meeting so many terrific fans. I know this all sounds like fun, but there was plenty of times I was so exhausted I felt like I was losing myself. But I guess what kept me going was knowing how much my mom sacrificed for me to chase my dream, how hard my team worked to make this happen and just seeing the excited faces of my fans all around the world. Even in my worst moments, you all seem to lift me up.

Traveling has definitely opened my eyes to different cultures and the way people see things. It was a total trip (no pun intended) getting to sing to my Parisian fans in French. I think it blew their minds a little bit. Traveling has taught me more than any school ever taught me. And I've done more geography than most students get.

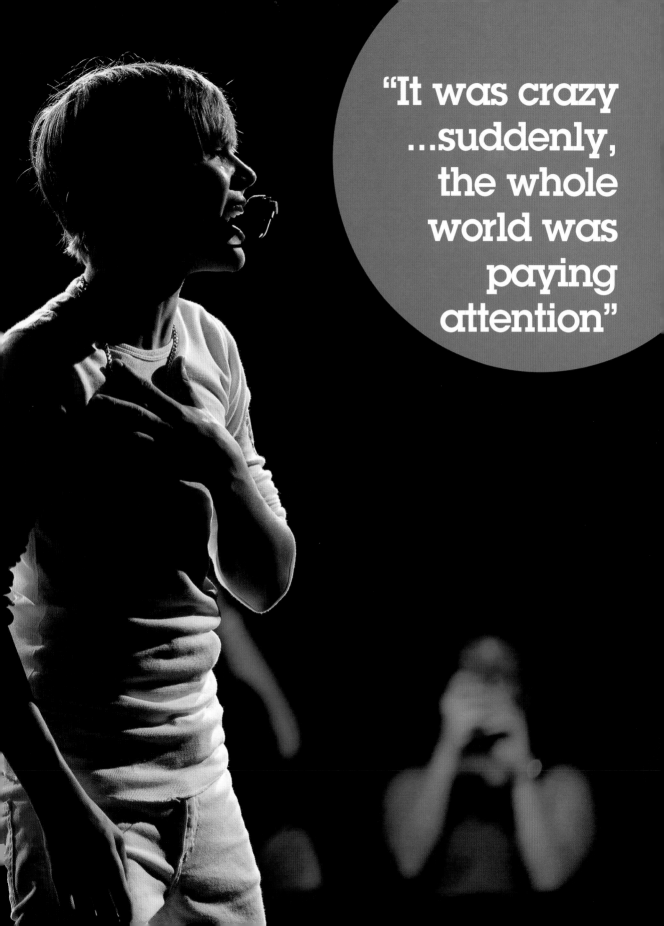

"It was crazy ...suddenly, the whole world was paying attention"

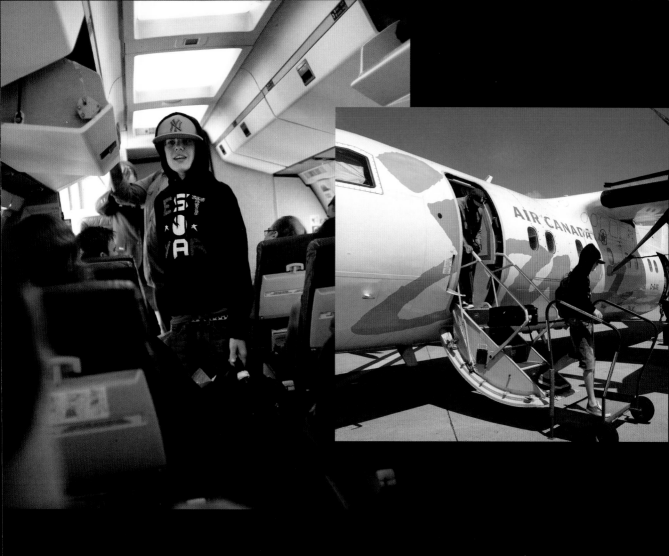

"Traveling has definitely
opened my eyes to different
cultures and the way people

BREAK A LEG

In November 2009, I was invited to open for Taylor Swift at Wembley Arena in London. It was the biggest crowd I'd seen so far – over twelve thousand people. I wasn't nervous about performing, just incredibly thrilled to be on there with Taylor in front of so many gorgeous fans.

Before I went on, Usher coached me on how to use the incredible energy that comes off a crowd that size. 'Allow the crowd to work with you. They want to sing with you. I know you're fighting to get each and every lyric out, but, a lot of times, give it to them. Allow them to be part of it, you know? Because they are. This is a connection. They're connecting to you. Take your time with it, man. Make it personal. You're here, you're there – that's their moment, that touch, that relationship.'

I was stoked. I got out there and did my set, and it went great. Tay James was lighting the fire for our last number before the encore.

'When I say Justin, you say Bieber! Justin!'

'Bieber!'

'Justin!'

'Bieber!'

'When I say one, you say time! One!'

'Time!'

'One!'

'Time!'

justinbieber About to hit the stage in London at Wembley. Let's do this! Thanks for the invite

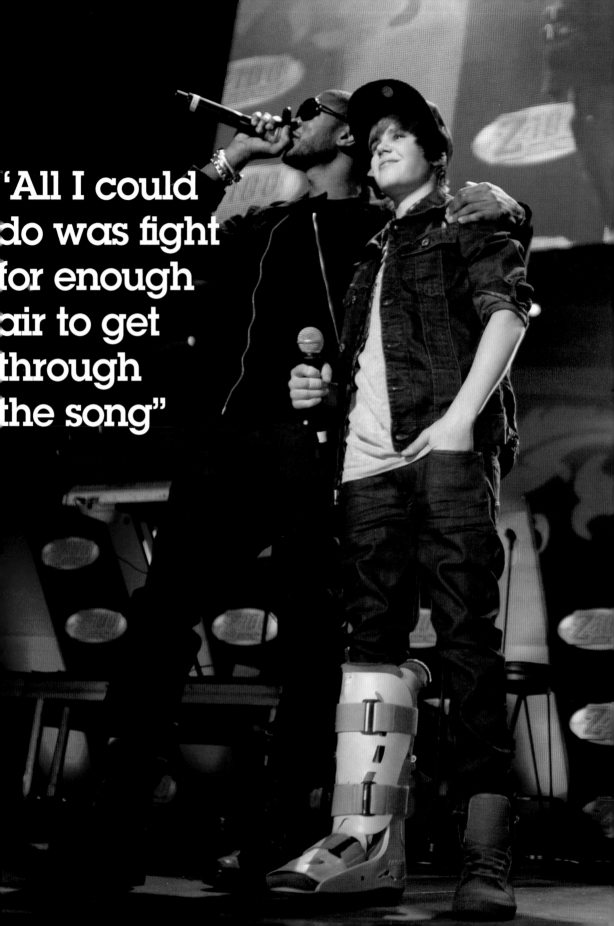

"All I could do was fight for enough air to get through the song"

That energy Usher talked about was a living, breathing thing — times twelve thousand. I started down the ramp. My voice was strong, the moves felt solid, everything was right until I got to the end of the ramp and ended up just a couple inches from where I should have been. My foot rolled right to the edge of the ramp, and it felt like stepping on a railroad spike. Pain instantly ripped through the nerve endings from my big toe to the back of my neck. I'd broken my foot skateboarding the year before, so I knew immediately that this was seriously messed up.

My foot was broken.

In the middle of a song.

In front of twelve thousand people.

And Taylor Swift.

I won't tell you the words that went through my head. Meanwhile, the song kept coming out of my mouth, part muscle memory, part hardcore hockey kid, part Mama Jan training automatically kicking in. I kept singing, and the crowd kept going crazy, but people onstage started looking at me like they knew something was wrong. There was no way I could dance like I normally do. I was probably dancing like that spazzy chemistry teacher who chaperoned your last homecoming dance. Every step was another spike. It took everything I had to keep from screaming. All I could do was fight for enough air to get through the song.

Longest three minutes of my life. I pushed through to the end, and Dan brought it home. I managed to wave and thank everybody

as I limped off, but, once I got backstage, I howled like a dog. I won't lie, I was crying. It was just so much pain. Kenny scooped me up and started looking toward the green room, yelling over his shoulder, 'Get the paramedics!'

People backstage were freaking out. 'What's wrong?'

Scooter dove into the fray, and my mom was right behind him. 'Justin? Oh, my God! What happened?'

I groaned something that basically meant 'I broke my friggin' foot again.'

Scooter threw the green room door open, and Kenny plopped me on the sofa.

'Are you sure?' he said. 'Maybe you just twisted—'

'Aagh! Don't touch it!'

'Okay. Okay. You're okay.' He whipped out his iPhone to troubleshoot the first aid and find out what an American manager is supposed to do with a wounded Canadian singer in England.

Taylor was so sweet. She was moments from going on. The fans were out there waiting for her — twelve-thousand people chanting her name — but first she dashed back to see if I was okay. She's a cool person and a real pro. She genuinely cared that I was hurt, but she had the show to do.

'Hang in there, Justin. You'll be all right.' She gave me a solid hug and was out the door, running for the stage. Her mom stayed with my mom, who was a little unnerved by the whole thing. We located a hospital where I could get X-rays and a cast. Not exactly the after-party I'd dreamed of when I imagined playing my biggest show so far.

The next day, we went to an orthopedist who fitted me with an Aircast. On the outside, the hard shell looked like a stormtrooper boot from *Star Wars*. Inside, it had air cells that inflated to fit tight and immobilize my foot and ankle. This made it possible for me to continue performing, but, still, immobility and I are not good together. It drove me crazy that I couldn't skateboard or play soccer or skate or much of anything else for eight weeks. I did all the media stuff and the shows, but I was hopping around on my one good foot like some peg-legged pirate.

To summarize the whole broken-foot incident: it sucked.

For one thing, it really hurt. For another thing, I was slated to perform at 'Christmas in Washington 2009', along with Usher, Mary J. Blige, Neil Diamond and a lot of other amazing performers.

The night of the performance in Washington — I'll admit it — I was nervous. It was a huge honor. And I wasn't keen on the idea of getting up in front of President Obama and a massive television audience in my stormtrooper boot.

'I'm taking the Aircast off,' I told Mom and Scooter.

They both said, 'No, you're not!'

'Okay,' I said.

As soon as they walked out of the dressing room, I took it off and pulled my shoe out of my backpack. It felt a little strange at first, but I wasn't even thinking about it when I stepped out in front of the President and First Lady. I sang the great old Stevie Wonder song 'Someday at Christmas', then went back to the dressing room and quickly put the Aircast on before Mom could get to me. How about this for the greatest dodge of all time? 'Sorry, Mom. Can't talk now. Chillin' with Mary J. Blige and Mrs Obama.'

Even with all that going on, Mom and I made sure that we were back in Stratford at Christmas, ready to play the gift exchange game and snarf down plenty of Grandma's turkey and gravy. Some things never change.

That was the Christmas where I met that girl and made out with her furiously for several days straight and we went on to have the most romantic relationship in the history of man. Wait…that did not happen. But I did have fun just pranking you right there while you sat excitedly in your room reading about it. Sorry, I just had to have a little fun. Next chapter. AW, C'MON!!

CHAPTER 7

JUST THE BEGINNING

justinbieber yeah super stoked. its crazy. last year i was watching the Grammys now i get to be there. get to meet some of my heroes. Insane

8:19 PM Jan 30th via web

January starts the awards season in the music industry, and in the United States the biggest, most epic and most prestigious is the Grammys, of course. Seeing that I'd just gotten my album out five weeks before the end of the year, we weren't expecting to be included, but I was asked to present with Ke$ha who was also a new artist that year.

The two of us were to promo this upcoming interactive fan thing. Viewers were invited to vote on which song Bon Jovi would perform later in the show. Cool concept, right? I had to read a little blurb off the teleprompter: 'You can still go to CBS dot com slash Grammys to vote on which song Bon Jovi will be playing in a matter of minutes.'

But you know me – I can't resist a good prank. After the long parade through all the media on the red carpet, having my mind blown every five seconds by the amazing people I was meeting, I got up there with Ke$ha and, to my delight, sitting in the front

"You know me...I can't resist a good prank"

"It was an amazing night I'll never forget...it totally blew my mind"

row was my longtime crush, Beyoncé. She was so beautiful. Sorry, Jay-Z, I'm not trying to hit on your girl but I'm just saying.

I decided to go for it, so rather than saying 'Bon Jovi', I said Beyoncé's name instead.

'I mean – I mean Bon Jovi. Bon Jovi,' I stammered. 'Sorry. Beyoncé's always on my mind.'

Even though I did it on purpose, everyone in the audience thought I'd genuinely messed up. Gotcha! Even Beyoncé herself thought it was a mistake so she consoled me when I met her backstage. Oh sweet, sweet victory! Ha ha.

It was an amazing night I'll never forget. I got to meet so many of my idols like Lionel Richie, Dave Matthews, Quincy Jones, Lil Wayne and Mary J. Blige – and Jay-Z and Beyoncé of course. It totally blew my mind.

The main music awards in Canada are the Junos and the MuchMusic Video Awards. I was nominated for New Artist of the Year at the Junos, but Drake edged me out. (Good game, Drake.) Miley Cyrus hosted the MuchMusic Awards, so that was win-win, no matter how you slice it. I was nominated and won UR Fave New Artist and UR Fave Video. I had two songs nominated for International Video of the Year by a Canadian, so I actually beat myself. (Good game, Bieb!)

That was kind of a CHUCK NORRIS moment for me.

NEVER SAY NEVER

Usher reminds me on a regular basis that there will be a whole lot of awards given out during the course of my career. Some will go to me, some won't. It's an honor to be nominated and awesome to win, but you can't lose sight of the real honors and victories that happen off camera. Like this letter I got a couple weeks after the MMVAs:

June 15th 2010

Dear Justin,

I am writing to you to thank you for something you have no idea you did . . . you helped me get through chemo . . .

In October of 2009, I was scheduled to have surgery and found out afterwards that I had a malignant tumor. It was removed, but my parents were told that I had to go through a few rounds of chemo just to be safe. As much as I found this devastating, I knew I had to fight it all the way. The day after your concert in Toronto at the Kool Haus, I went into sick kids hospital to start my first treatment. I was very scared of what I was going to be put thru and how my body would react. The only thing that kept me going (other than my mother being by my side) was the fact that I was on stage with you the night before. You sang to me and afterwards gave me the hat right off your head.

Your hat and your pictures decorated my hospital room each time I went for my treatments. I educated the doctors and nurses about Bieber trivia and many times even sang them a few of your songs. When I found the poking and prodding too much to bear, I simply looked at the picture of you and me on stage, smiled and got thru one more ordeal. I remembered you saying those famous words to me, 'only you shawty' and everything seemed easier to handle. Words can never express how much that one seemingly little gesture helped me overcome the terrible disease my body was fighting.

I am sure one day I will have the opportunity to meet and thank you personally, but until then,

Your most sincere fan,

Sabrina Moreino

"Every one of my fans is so special to me"

This letter really touched my heart. Sabrina says when she lost all her hair during chemo, she wore the cap I gave her. It reminded me of that old Rascal Flatts song about Sarah Beth, a girl who's going through chemo and loses her hair, but when she's at the prom, dancing with a guy who cares about her, 'for a moment, she's not afraid.' I can't tell you what it means to me that I was part of that moment for Sabrina. She's out of the woods now and on her way to a long, healthy life, but I'll keep praying for her. People like Sabrina and so many fans I've met along the road have taught me to never forget to *Never Say Never*.

Every one of my fans is so special to me. I love being in the studio, but not as much as I love performing live, because that's when I get to connect with you. One of my favorite moments in every show is when I get to walk downstage, look right into those beautiful eyes and tell you,

 If you need me, I'll come running from a thousand miles away...

A lot of you have seen my adorable little three-year-old fan, Cody. Someone posted a hilarious video of her crying because she couldn't see me. Two nights before my sixteenth birthday, I did *Jimmy Kimmel Live!* in Los Angeles and got to meet Cody and her family backstage. You should have seen her face when I walked in the door! (Seriously, check it out on YouTube. Her eyes got as big as baseballs.) Funny thing is, I was just as excited to meet Cody. Her YouTube video had us smiling for weeks.

A couple of days later, we rocked the house with an amazing sixteenth-birthday party. Everyone was wondering if I'd celebrate by doing something crazy, but all I wanted was to spend time with my family, my friends and my team. We rented a house and filled it with the most incredible food, played basketball, swam, sang karaoke and even did sumo wrestling! It felt so good to just be a kid and be surrounded by people who truly love me for me. To top it all off, after that party I flew back to Canada and spent some quality time with my family there. And what did we do? We went bowling. I guess it's not as extravagant as you might think from a recording artist, but at the end of the day, I'm still a regular kid. I don't expect, nor do I want, anyone to treat me any differently.

justinbieber Thanks to everyone for the birthday wishes. u guys all changed my life and are giving me a great birthday. appreciate it

2:44 PM Mar 1st via web

"We rocked the house with an amazing sixteenth-birthday party. We rented a house and filled it with the most incredible food, played basketball, swam, sang karaoke and even did sumo wrestling"

PERMIT ME

Even though I don't want to be given special treatment, I guess some things are a little bit different for me as I was surprised to be given a Range Rover for my sixteenth birthday.

AW C'MON!

I was feeling like it was pretty pathetic that I couldn't drive it because I still hadn't got my permit. I sneaked a trip around the block one day, and Mom came unglued at me.

'Justin! You know you can't be driving that car. You don't have a license. You don't even have a permit.'

How lame is that? Sixteen and still hadn't found time to get my permit.

'I should have had it a year ago,' I told Mom. 'At this rate, I won't have it till I'm thirty.'

'Okay,' she said. 'We'll clear a day next week. Top priority is you and me at the DMV.'

I cleared the day with the team. The day arrived, and I texted everyone who ever owned a cellphone to tell them I was getting my driver's permit.

'Woo hoo! Driver's permit! Forthcoming today! Freedom imminent!'

'Did you study for the test?' Scooter asked.

'Sure. Yeah. Well . . . you know . . . I thought about it. About driving, I mean. I've got it down cold. Don't worry. I won't fail the test.'

'You should probably study up a little, Justin.'

'I said I won't fail the test.'

'Some people fail the test because they didn't look at the rule book.'

'Dude. I won't fail the test.'

So I went and failed the friggin' test.

I walked in the door, fully expecting to walk out with a driver's permit, hop in the driver's seat and begin my life as a free man. Instead, I stood there staring at the woman behind the counter, trying not to hear what she was saying.

'Oopsy,' she smiled. 'Close but no cigar. You missed it by one question.'

'What? No...no way.'

She handed me a piece of paper that was not a driver's permit.

'Take a little time to review these correct answers and come back in thirty days.'

'Thirty days?'

Was she kidding me? I didn't even know what country I'd be in thirty days from then. All I knew was I'd be thirty days older. With no driver's permit.

I mumbled some kind of thank you, shoved my shades

on my face, and pulled my hood as low as I could. Mom was waiting out in the lobby area, and she didn't have to ask me what happened on the way out.

    'Oh, Justin . . . it's okay. It'll be fine. You can take it again–'

    'Let's just go,' I hissed.

    Outside in the parking lot, it was pouring down rain, and Mom dove into the car. In the driver's seat. Screw this, man. C'mon. This was so freaking unfair. I couldn't stand it. I started walking. Walking ten miles in the rain seemed easier than getting in the

"It felt like every car that drove by was taunting me"

passenger seat when my whole heart was set on driving home.

Mom opened her window a crack and yelled, 'Justin! You're getting drenched. Get in the car.'

But I felt like I was going to cry, and there was no way I was getting in that friggin' passenger seat, bawling like a ten-year-old. She kept calling out for me as I walked to the corner of the parking lot and stood by the street. It felt like every car that drove by was taunting me.

Nee-nur, nee-nur. We can drive, and you can't!

Some girl drove by, yakking on her cellphone and putting on mascara as she weaved down the boulevard, but she sure as heck had a driver's license, didn't she? A little old lady passed by doing twelve miles per hour. She could barely see over the steering wheel of her Cadillac, but she obviously had no problem passing the stinking test. Some big dude cruised by in a pickup truck, smoking a cigarette, which he tossed out onto the street as if the world was his friggin' ashtray. He gets to drive, and I don't?

'Aaugh! I hate you!' I bellowed after him. It felt so good, I bellowed at the next guy. 'I hate you, too! And I hate you! And I hate you! I hate you!'

Mom sat in the car while I vented my frustration on the traffic. Every once in a while, she'd crack the window and call,

'Justin, that's enough. Justin? Seriously. Get in the car – now.'

I finally got in, soaking wet. Justin Bieber, world's newest pop star without a driver's permit. Later that day, Scooter and Kenny came to take me somewhere, and I told him, 'This blows.'

'Yeah, it does,' he said. 'Thirty days goes fast, though. You'll get it next time.'

'I failed it by one question, and when I looked at the answers – this one right here – I know I had this one right.' I pulled the crumpled paper from my hoody. 'When permitted to turn right at a red light, you should (a) proceed to turn right, (b) slow down before making the right turn, or (c) come to a complete stop, then proceed with the right turn.'

'Dude, you come to a complete stop and then turn,' said Scooter.

'What? That's bull! Nobody ever comes to a complete stop.'

'Well, they're supposed to.'

'You never stop.'

'Yes, I do. I always stop.'

'Dude, I've been in the car with you ten million times, and never once did you come to a complete stop before turning right.'

'That's true, man,' Kenny said helpfully. 'You never stop, Scooter.'

'Well, that's – I'm just – okay, but it doesn't matter what I do,' said Scooter. 'What matters is the law, and the law is that you

"There's always so much laughter at the end of the road"

come to a complete stop, and now you know that. You'll take the test again, and maybe take a look at the book next time.'

I shoved the paper back in my pocket, thinking, Dang! Why didn't I study for the freakin' test? But out loud, I said, 'This is bull, man. This blows.'

'I know,' said Scooter. 'I failed it my first time, too.'

'I failed it three times,' said Kenny. 'Fourth time was the charm.'

Scooter and I looked at him for a minute, and then we all fell out laughing our heads off.

'Four times,' said Scooter. 'I admire your tenacity, Kenny. If that was me I'd still be riding a bicycle.'

We couldn't stop laughing. I guess the lesson I learned from that day is that no matter how bad I think things might be, there's always some laughter at the end of the road. You've just got to look for it.

justinbieber Why do u drive on a parkway and park in the driveway. Its messed up

7:37 PM Jun 2nd via Twitter for BlackBerry®

PUNKED

I took the test thirty days later and got the permit, so it was cool in the end, but what was not cool was my voice when I woke up the morning after yelling at traffic in the rain. I could hardly talk, let alone sing. I could barely croak. Any time I get sick or my voice gets wrecked from horsing around at a party or screaming my lungs out at a basketball or hockey game, everybody acts like it's the end of the world. Mama Jan comes in and takes over.

'Voice rest. Not a word.'

She lays down the law, and she's not kidding. I'm not allowed to talk or sing at all until she says it's okay. Then she works with me like a drill sergeant until everything's back to normal. Meanwhile, Scooter and his team have to scramble around and reschedule everything I was supposed to be doing as far as interviews or recording or anything like that is concerned.

This particular time, I was supposed to have done this celebrity playlist thing for YouTube, and the person we'd promised to do it for was kind of bent out of shape when Scooter called to tell her it wasn't happening. We were coming up on the release date for *My World 2.0*, and we needed everyone in our corner, so Scooter told her, 'It's cool. We'll work something out.'

Later that day, he came over and said, 'Here's what we're gonna do. You know how kung fu movies are dubbed over in

"I could hardly talk let alone sing"

English? Like the skinny little guy's mouth is moving and this big, growling voice is coming out, but it doesn't match up. You just sit there in the chair and move your lips, and I'll do the voice.'

'Yeah, man, that's—'

'Shut up! No talking.'

'But what are you going to say?'

'I've got the list you made. I'll just come up with something.'

I nodded. A rep from Def Jam set up the camera, and I parked myself in a chair across the room from Scooter, who had my playlist of favorite videos in hand. On cue, I made a kung foo face and moved my mouth, and Scooter did his growling voiceover.

'Thank you for watching the premiere of my new video 'Never Let You Go'. Now we will go to my celebrity playlist. Number one, you've already seen it. 'Never Let You Go'. The next video… ah, the great CHUCK NORRIS, roundhouse kicking champion. He's fighting a bear. Who fights a bear? Only CHUCK NORRIS. The bear ran away. I love this video. Next video. Cody crying. Ah, young Padawan Cody. She cried because she could not see me the entire day. I met her later on. You can find that on YouTube, too, but, for now, watch her cry. Crying is music to my ears. The next video . . . hold on. Let me remember what it is.'

Scooter looked at the list but couldn't read my sloppy

"We love
to punk
each other"

handwriting. He showed it to the rep and said, 'What is it?'

She managed to squeak, 'Legaci'. On camera, I was dying, trying not to laugh.

'Ah. The next video is my new background singers, Legaci. They were discovered by me, Justin Bieber, by singing my song "Baby". Check them out. It's actually pretty good. I like them. I will not slay them.'

The rep and I cracked up laughing, so we had to stop for a minute.

'Dude, no laughing,' Scooter said. 'Knock it off.'

'Okay. I'm good.'

'No talking!'

'Fine!'

'Shut up!'

I rolled my eyes, and the rep started recording again.

'Hi. I am Justin Bieber, and I am back. I was just working out.'

I started to lose it again, but Scooter was looking at me like Do. Not. Laugh.

'I'm going to give you one more great video for my celebrity playlist. This one is of the biggest snakes in the world. It is a great video. Watch it till the end. It will slay you. Now. Make sure you buy my new album, *My World part 2.0.* It is . . . the ish. Get out of my face. I am Justin Bieber. The master. Vlaaaugh!'

Cut. Cut. Cut. We were laughing so hard.

Sorry, Mama Jan, I couldn't help it. That was awesome.

As much as we love to punk each other, we laugh a lot about the crazy stuff that gets spread around (sometimes in fun, sometimes not) to punk me and my fans. Usually, we laugh it off, but every once in a while I've just gotta say something . . .

justinbieber let's take some time to answer some crazy rumors…really fun…

2.43 PM Jun 29th via web

justinbieber ONE…Im not dead. I had to check on this one…but it turns out Im alive

2.44 PM Jun 29th via web

justinbieber TWO…my mom is a moral woman…let's just leave that one for what it is…because that rumor just grossed and wierded me out…

2.46 PM Jun 29th via web

justinbieber THREE…I have not joined the Illuminati or any other cult. Im a christian and I pray before every show and am thankful for every blessing

2.47 PM Jun 29th via web

justinbieber FOUR...Im not Peter Pan... Im growing up and my voice will change but no worries Jan Smith is the greatest vocal coach ever . . . stronger than ever!

2.50 PM Jun 29th via web

justinbieber SIX...I am not 10 feet tall and I dont shoot fire balls from my arse...that was BraveHeart

2.54 PM Jun 29th via web

justinbieber SEVEN...yes we did skip 5...why??? I dont know...5 was chillin and didnt want to join the fun

2.56 PM Jun 29th via web

justinbieber EIGHT...asherroth is not my real big bro... he is just the big bro in friendship...we have Bromance.

2.59 PM Jun 29th via web

justinbieber NINE...Im home schooled and not going to a high school next year in every city we have visited

3.00 PM Jun 29th via web

justinbieber and TEN...No CHUCK NORRIS is not my real father . . . although he did birth to Hercules

3.02 PM Jun 29th via web

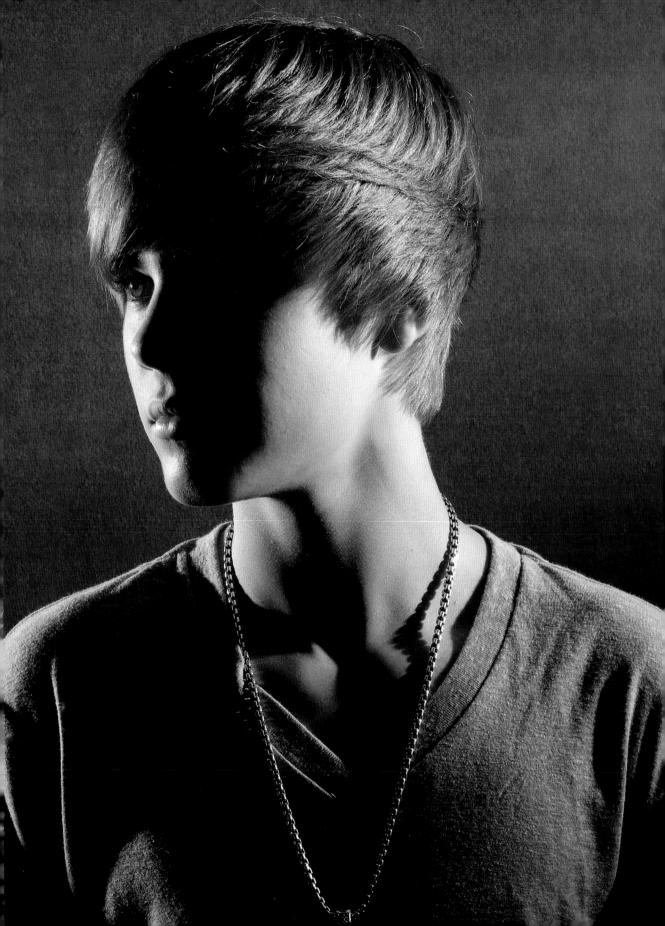

LET THE MUSIC BEGIN

HARTFORD, CONNECTICUT
TUESDAY, 22 JUNE 2010
8.30PM

The XL Center is rockin' with noise and energy. The Stunners light it up, and Sean Kingston burns it down. Backstage in my dressing room, I'm drumming my hands on my lap. The words to my latest single keep playing in my head.

 I never thought that I could walk through fire
Never thought that I could take a burn
Never had the strength to take it higher
Until I reached the point of no return . . .

Ryan says, 'It's time.'

My team gather in a tight huddle. Mom thanks God for all the blessings that have poured out on us. Mama Jan prays that my voice will be empowered with love. I pray for the safety of me and my dance crew and everyone above and below the stage. Dan leads us in ancient Hebrew prayer Scooter taught us.

'Sh'ma Yis'ra'eil Adonai Eloheinu Adonai echad.' (Hear, oh Israel, that the Lord is our God, the Lord is One.)

We head for the stage entrance, Kenny and Scooter blazing the trail. Mom is two steps behind us. Even when I can't see her, I know she's there. Usher walks beside me, one strong hand on my shoulder. He leans in close to my ear so I can hear him over the jet-engine scream of twenty thousand fans.

'First step to forever, man.'

And then my music begins.

THANK YOU

This is just the beginning. Thanks for making a small town kid's dreams come true. Never Say Never. Love you.